C-4981   CAREER EXAMINATION SERIES

This is your
PASSBOOK for...

Supervisor Electrician

Test Preparation Study Guide
Questions & Answers

COPYRIGHT NOTICE

This book is SOLELY intended for, is sold ONLY to, and its use is RESTRICTED to individual, bona fide applicants or candidates who qualify by virtue of having seriously filed applications for appropriate license, certificate, professional and/or promotional advancement, higher school matriculation, scholarship, or other legitimate requirements of education and/or governmental authorities.

This book is NOT intended for use, class instruction, tutoring, training, duplication, copying, reprinting, excerption, or adaptation, etc., by:

1) Other publishers
2) Proprietors and/or Instructors of "Coaching" and/or Preparatory Courses
3) Personnel and/or Training Divisions of commercial, industrial, and governmental organizations
4) Schools, colleges, or universities and/or their departments and staffs, including teachers and other personnel
5) Testing Agencies or Bureaus
6) Study groups which seek by the purchase of a single volume to copy and/or duplicate and/or adapt this material for use by the group as a whole without having purchased individual volumes for each of the members of the group
7) Et al.

Such persons would be in violation of appropriate Federal and State statutes.

PROVISION OF LICENSING AGREEMENTS – Recognized educational, commercial, industrial, and governmental institutions and organizations, and others legitimately engaged in educational pursuits, including training, testing, and measurement activities, may address request for a licensing agreement to the copyright owners, who will determine whether, and under what conditions, including fees and charges, the materials in this book may be used them. In other words, a licensing facility exists for the legitimate use of the material in this book on other than an individual basis. However, it is asseverated and affirmed here that the material in this book CANNOT be used without the receipt of the express permission of such a licensing agreement from the Publishers. Inquiries re licensing should be addressed to the company, attention rights and permissions department.

All rights reserved, including the right of reproduction in whole or in part, in any form or by any means, electronic or mechanical, including photocopying, recording, or by any information storage and retrieval system, without permission in writing from the Publisher.

Copyright © 2024 by
National Learning Corporation

212 Michael Drive, Syosset, NY 11791
(516) 921-8888 • www.passbooks.com
E-mail: info@passbooks.com

PUBLISHED IN THE UNITED STATES OF AMERICA

PASSBOOK® SERIES

THE *PASSBOOK® SERIES* has been created to prepare applicants and candidates for the ultimate academic battlefield – the examination room.

At some time in our lives, each and every one of us may be required to take an examination – for validation, matriculation, admission, qualification, registration, certification, or licensure.

Based on the assumption that every applicant or candidate has met the basic formal educational standards, has taken the required number of courses, and read the necessary texts, the *PASSBOOK® SERIES* furnishes the one special preparation which may assure passing with confidence, instead of failing with insecurity. Examination questions – together with answers – are furnished as the basic vehicle for study so that the mysteries of the examination and its compounding difficulties may be eliminated or diminished by a sure method.

This book is meant to help you pass your examination provided that you qualify and are serious in your objective.

The entire field is reviewed through the huge store of content information which is succinctly presented through a provocative and challenging approach – the question-and-answer method.

A climate of success is established by furnishing the correct answers at the end of each test.

You soon learn to recognize types of questions, forms of questions, and patterns of questioning. You may even begin to anticipate expected outcomes.

You perceive that many questions are repeated or adapted so that you can gain acute insights, which may enable you to score many sure points.

You learn how to confront new questions, or types of questions, and to attack them confidently and work out the correct answers.

You note objectives and emphases, and recognize pitfalls and dangers, so that you may make positive educational adjustments.

Moreover, you are kept fully informed in relation to new concepts, methods, practices, and directions in the field.

You discover that you are actually taking the examination all the time: you are preparing for the examination by "taking" an examination, not by reading extraneous and/or supererogatory textbooks.

In short, this PASSBOOK®, used directedly, should be an important factor in helping you to pass your test.

SUPERVISOR ELECTRICIAN

DUTIES
Under general supervision, Supervisor Electricians supervise electricians and other assigned personnel in the installation, repair, replacement and maintenance of apparatus, equipment and electric wiring circuits for buildings, bridges and elevated structures and/or traffic control systems according to the provisions of the Administrative Code and electrical practice in the City. Supervisor Electricians prepare and are responsible for the work of electricians, electrician's helpers, and other assigned personnel in altering, repairing and maintaining appliances, equipment and wiring circuits in electrical installations for light, heat and power in or on buildings and/or traffic control systems; make decisions relative to work procedures; prepare work schedules and make work assignments; make field inspections in connection with electrical installations and components of systems relative to work progress or need for alterations, maintenance and repairs; prepare job orders and tool and material requisitions; supervise the complete operation of the department shop; consult with staff personnel, contractors, inspectors, and manufacturers' representatives in connection with department work; keep records and make reports; and operate a motor vehicle or related transport equipment to access work sites in the performance of assigned duties. All Supervisor Electricians perform related work.

SCOPE OF THE EXAMINATION
The multiple-choice test is designed to assess the extent to which candidates have certain knowledges and abilities determined to be important to the performance of the tasks of a Supervisor Electrician. Tasks categories to be tested are as follows: repair, installation, and maintenance; safety; interpretation, review, and revision of drawings; supervising staff; and administrative duties. The test may include questions on single-phase and three-phase electricity; methods and procedures for the installation, repair, and maintenance of high and/or low tension electrical systems and equipment for light, heat, power, fire alarm, and/or communication (i.e. voice, data, and video); AC & DC circuitry, control systems, and machinery; applied electronics; electrical calculations; reading and interpreting electrical drawings and specifications; safe working practices and procedures; proper use and selection of tools, fittings, materials, measuring instruments and meters used in the electrical trade; electrical code; and other related areas.

The test may also include questions requiring the use of any of the following abilities:

Analytical Thinking: Analyzing information and using logic to address specific work-related issues and problems; involves the identification of problems, not implementation of solutions. Example: A Supervisor Electrician might use this ability when judging when it is appropriate to call a supporting agency to assist in solving a problem or completing a job.

Judgment & Decision-Making: Reviewing information to develop and evaluate the relative costs and benefits of potential solutions to problems and choosing the most appropriate one; implementing a course of action determined by thinking analytically. While similar to Planning & Organizing, Judgment and Decision-Making are typically applied over a shorter time frame. Example: A Supervisor Electrician might use this ability when reviewing plans and judging how to lower labor cost by using less manpower or equipment to complete the job.

Planning & Organizing: Establishing a method of execution to accomplish a specific goal over an extended period of time; determining appropriate assignments and allocation of resources. Example: A Supervisor Electrician might use this ability when assigning tasks and job assignments.

Management of Material Resources: Obtaining and seeing to the appropriate use of equipment, facilities and materials needed to do certain work; managing the things needed for work to be accomplished. Example: A Supervisor Electrician might use this ability when scheduling personnel, coordinating delivery of materials and assuring the transport of the appropriate equipment.

Management of Personnel Resources: Motivating, developing and directing people as they work, identifying the best people for the job; managing employees needed to accomplish tasks. Example: A Supervisor Electrician might use this ability when working with an employee's expertise and strengths to complete a job.

Written Comprehension: Understanding the information and ideas presented in written sentences and paragraphs in work-related documents. Example: A Supervisor Electrician might use this ability when reading and comprehending emails that require action, such as expense reports or sending an employee to a job site.

Written Expression: Appropriately communicating information and ideas in written words and sentences so intended audience will understand. Example: A Supervisor Electrician might use this ability when responding to an email to a Supervisor.

Attention to Detail: Being careful about detail and thorough in completing work tasks. Example: A Supervisor Electrician might use this ability when assuring that code compliance is a priority by focusing on safe, neat, and accurate work.

HOW TO TAKE A TEST

I. YOU MUST PASS AN EXAMINATION

A. WHAT EVERY CANDIDATE SHOULD KNOW

Examination applicants often ask us for help in preparing for the written test. What can I study in advance? What kinds of questions will be asked? How will the test be given? How will the papers be graded?

As an applicant for a civil service examination, you may be wondering about some of these things. Our purpose here is to suggest effective methods of advance study and to describe civil service examinations.

Your chances for success on this examination can be increased if you know how to prepare. Those "pre-examination jitters" can be reduced if you know what to expect. You can even experience an adventure in good citizenship if you know why civil service exams are given.

B. WHY ARE CIVIL SERVICE EXAMINATIONS GIVEN?

Civil service examinations are important to you in two ways. As a citizen, you want public jobs filled by employees who know how to do their work. As a job seeker, you want a fair chance to compete for that job on an equal footing with other candidates. The best-known means of accomplishing this two-fold goal is the competitive examination.

Exams are widely publicized throughout the nation. They may be administered for jobs in federal, state, city, municipal, town or village governments or agencies.

Any citizen may apply, with some limitations, such as the age or residence of applicants. Your experience and education may be reviewed to see whether you meet the requirements for the particular examination. When these requirements exist, they are reasonable and applied consistently to all applicants. Thus, a competitive examination may cause you some uneasiness now, but it is your privilege and safeguard.

C. HOW ARE CIVIL SERVICE EXAMS DEVELOPED?

Examinations are carefully written by trained technicians who are specialists in the field known as "psychological measurement," in consultation with recognized authorities in the field of work that the test will cover. These experts recommend the subject matter areas or skills to be tested; only those knowledges or skills important to your success on the job are included. The most reliable books and source materials available are used as references. Together, the experts and technicians judge the difficulty level of the questions.

Test technicians know how to phrase questions so that the problem is clearly stated. Their ethics do not permit "trick" or "catch" questions. Questions may have been tried out on sample groups, or subjected to statistical analysis, to determine their usefulness.

Written tests are often used in combination with performance tests, ratings of training and experience, and oral interviews. All of these measures combine to form the best-known means of finding the right person for the right job.

II. HOW TO PASS THE WRITTEN TEST

A. *NATURE OF THE EXAMINATION*

To prepare intelligently for civil service examinations, you should know how they differ from school examinations you have taken. In school you were assigned certain definite pages to read or subjects to cover. The examination questions were quite detailed and usually emphasized memory. Civil service exams, on the other hand, try to discover your present ability to perform the duties of a position, plus your potentiality to learn these duties. In other words, a civil service exam attempts to predict how successful you will be. Questions cover such a broad area that they cannot be as minute and detailed as school exam questions.

In the public service similar kinds of work, or positions, are grouped together in one "class." This process is known as *position-classification*. All the positions in a class are paid according to the salary range for that class. One class title covers all of these positions, and they are all tested by the same examination.

B. *FOUR BASIC STEPS*

1) Study the announcement

How, then, can you know what subjects to study? Our best answer is: "Learn as much as possible about the class of positions for which you've applied." The exam will test the knowledge, skills and abilities needed to do the work.

Your most valuable source of information about the position you want is the official exam announcement. This announcement lists the training and experience qualifications. Check these standards and apply only if you come reasonably close to meeting them.

The brief description of the position in the examination announcement offers some clues to the subjects which will be tested. Think about the job itself. Review the duties in your mind. Can you perform them, or are there some in which you are rusty? Fill in the blank spots in your preparation.

Many jurisdictions preview the written test in the exam announcement by including a section called "Knowledge and Abilities Required," "Scope of the Examination," or some similar heading. Here you will find out specifically what fields will be tested.

2) Review your own background

Once you learn in general what the position is all about, and what you need to know to do the work, ask yourself which subjects you already know fairly well and which need improvement. You may wonder whether to concentrate on improving your strong areas or on building some background in your fields of weakness. When the announcement has specified "some knowledge" or "considerable knowledge," or has used adjectives like "beginning principles of..." or "advanced ... methods," you can get a clue as to the number and difficulty of questions to be asked in any given field. More questions, and hence broader coverage, would be included for those subjects which are more important in the work. Now weigh your strengths and weaknesses against the job requirements and prepare accordingly.

3) Determine the level of the position

Another way to tell how intensively you should prepare is to understand the level of the job for which you are applying. Is it the entering level? In other words, is this the position in which beginners in a field of work are hired? Or is it an intermediate or advanced level? Sometimes this is indicated by such words as "Junior" or "Senior" in the class title. Other jurisdictions use Roman numerals to designate the level – Clerk I, Clerk II, for example. The word "Supervisor" sometimes appears in the title. If the level is not indicated by the title, check the description of duties. Will you be working under very close supervision, or will you have responsibility for independent decisions in this work?

4) Choose appropriate study materials

Now that you know the subjects to be examined and the relative amount of each subject to be covered, you can choose suitable study materials. For beginning level jobs, or even advanced ones, if you have a pronounced weakness in some aspect of your training, read a modern, standard textbook in that field. Be sure it is up to date and has general coverage. Such books are normally available at your library, and the librarian will be glad to help you locate one. For entry-level positions, questions of appropriate difficulty are chosen – neither highly advanced questions, nor those too simple. Such questions require careful thought but not advanced training.

If the position for which you are applying is technical or advanced, you will read more advanced, specialized material. If you are already familiar with the basic principles of your field, elementary textbooks would waste your time. Concentrate on advanced textbooks and technical periodicals. Think through the concepts and review difficult problems in your field.

These are all general sources. You can get more ideas on your own initiative, following these leads. For example, training manuals and publications of the government agency which employs workers in your field can be useful, particularly for technical and professional positions. A letter or visit to the government department involved may result in more specific study suggestions, and certainly will provide you with a more definite idea of the exact nature of the position you are seeking.

III. KINDS OF TESTS

Tests are used for purposes other than measuring knowledge and ability to perform specified duties. For some positions, it is equally important to test ability to make adjustments to new situations or to profit from training. In others, basic mental abilities not dependent on information are essential. Questions which test these things may not appear as pertinent to the duties of the position as those which test for knowledge and information. Yet they are often highly important parts of a fair examination. For very general questions, it is almost impossible to help you direct your study efforts. What we can do is to point out some of the more common of these general abilities needed in public service positions and describe some typical questions.

1) General information

Broad, general information has been found useful for predicting job success in some kinds of work. This is tested in a variety of ways, from vocabulary lists to questions about current events. Basic background in some field of work, such as sociology or economics, may be sampled in a group of questions. Often these are principles which have become familiar to most persons through exposure rather than through formal training. It is difficult to advise you how to study for these questions; being alert to the world around you is our best suggestion.

2) Verbal ability

An example of an ability needed in many positions is verbal or language ability. Verbal ability is, in brief, the ability to use and understand words. Vocabulary and grammar tests are typical measures of this ability. Reading comprehension or paragraph interpretation questions are common in many kinds of civil service tests. You are given a paragraph of written material and asked to find its central meaning.

3) Numerical ability

Number skills can be tested by the familiar arithmetic problem, by checking paired lists of numbers to see which are alike and which are different, or by interpreting charts and graphs. In the latter test, a graph may be printed in the test booklet which you are asked to use as the basis for answering questions.

4) Observation

A popular test for law-enforcement positions is the observation test. A picture is shown to you for several minutes, then taken away. Questions about the picture test your ability to observe both details and larger elements.

5) Following directions

In many positions in the public service, the employee must be able to carry out written instructions dependably and accurately. You may be given a chart with several columns, each column listing a variety of information. The questions require you to carry out directions involving the information given in the chart.

6) Skills and aptitudes

Performance tests effectively measure some manual skills and aptitudes. When the skill is one in which you are trained, such as typing or shorthand, you can practice. These tests are often very much like those given in business school or high school courses. For many of the other skills and aptitudes, however, no short-time preparation can be made. Skills and abilities natural to you or that you have developed throughout your lifetime are being tested.

Many of the general questions just described provide all the data needed to answer the questions and ask you to use your reasoning ability to find the answers. Your best preparation for these tests, as well as for tests of facts and ideas, is to be at your physical and mental best. You, no doubt, have your own methods of getting into an exam-taking mood and keeping "in shape." The next section lists some ideas on this subject.

IV. KINDS OF QUESTIONS

Only rarely is the "essay" question, which you answer in narrative form, used in civil service tests. Civil service tests are usually of the short-answer type. Full instructions for answering these questions will be given to you at the examination. But in case this is your first experience with short-answer questions and separate answer sheets, here is what you need to know:

1) Multiple-choice Questions

Most popular of the short-answer questions is the "multiple choice" or "best answer" question. It can be used, for example, to test for factual knowledge, ability to solve problems or judgment in meeting situations found at work.

A multiple-choice question is normally one of three types—

- It can begin with an incomplete statement followed by several possible endings. You are to find the one ending which *best* completes the statement, although some of the others may not be entirely wrong.
- It can also be a complete statement in the form of a question which is answered by choosing one of the statements listed.

- It can be in the form of a problem – again you select the best answer.

Here is an example of a multiple-choice question with a discussion which should give you some clues as to the method for choosing the right answer:

When an employee has a complaint about his assignment, the action which will *best* help him overcome his difficulty is to
- A. discuss his difficulty with his coworkers
- B. take the problem to the head of the organization
- C. take the problem to the person who gave him the assignment
- D. say nothing to anyone about his complaint

In answering this question, you should study each of the choices to find which is best. Consider choice "A" – Certainly an employee may discuss his complaint with fellow employees, but no change or improvement can result, and the complaint remains unresolved. Choice "B" is a poor choice since the head of the organization probably does not know what assignment you have been given, and taking your problem to him is known as "going over the head" of the supervisor. The supervisor, or person who made the assignment, is the person who can clarify it or correct any injustice. Choice "C" is, therefore, correct. To say nothing, as in choice "D," is unwise. Supervisors have and interest in knowing the problems employees are facing, and the employee is seeking a solution to his problem.

2) True/False Questions

The "true/false" or "right/wrong" form of question is sometimes used. Here a complete statement is given. Your job is to decide whether the statement is right or wrong.

SAMPLE: A roaming cell-phone call to a nearby city costs less than a non-roaming call to a distant city.

This statement is wrong, or false, since roaming calls are more expensive.

This is not a complete list of all possible question forms, although most of the others are variations of these common types. You will always get complete directions for answering questions. Be sure you understand *how* to mark your answers – ask questions until you do.

V. RECORDING YOUR ANSWERS

Computer terminals are used more and more today for many different kinds of exams.
For an examination with very few applicants, you may be told to record your answers in the test booklet itself. Separate answer sheets are much more common. If this separate answer sheet is to be scored by machine – and this is often the case – it is highly important that you mark your answers correctly in order to get credit.

An electronic scoring machine is often used in civil service offices because of the speed with which papers can be scored. Machine-scored answer sheets must be marked with a pencil, which will be given to you. This pencil has a high graphite content which responds to the electronic scoring machine. As a matter of fact, stray dots may register as answers, so do not let your pencil rest on the answer sheet while you are pondering the correct answer. Also, if your pencil lead breaks or is otherwise defective, ask for another.

Since the answer sheet will be dropped in a slot in the scoring machine, be careful not to bend the corners or get the paper crumpled.

The answer sheet normally has five vertical columns of numbers, with 30 numbers to a column. These numbers correspond to the question numbers in your test booklet. After each number, going across the page are four or five pairs of dotted lines. These short dotted lines have small letters or numbers above them. The first two pairs may also have a "T" or "F" above the letters. This indicates that the first two pairs only are to be used if the questions are of the true-false type. If the questions are multiple choice, disregard the "T" and "F" and pay attention only to the small letters or numbers.

Answer your questions in the manner of the sample that follows:

32. The largest city in the United States is
    A. Washington, D.C.
    B. New York City
    C. Chicago
    D. Detroit
    E. San Francisco

1) Choose the answer you think is best. (New York City is the largest, so "B" is correct.)
2) Find the row of dotted lines numbered the same as the question you are answering. (Find row number 32)
3) Find the pair of dotted lines corresponding to the answer. (Find the pair of lines under the mark "B.")
4) Make a solid black mark between the dotted lines.

VI. BEFORE THE TEST

Common sense will help you find procedures to follow to get ready for an examination. Too many of us, however, overlook these sensible measures. Indeed, nervousness and fatigue have been found to be the most serious reasons why applicants fail to do their best on civil service tests. Here is a list of reminders:

- Begin your preparation early – Don't wait until the last minute to go scurrying around for books and materials or to find out what the position is all about.
- Prepare continuously – An hour a night for a week is better than an all-night cram session. This has been definitely established. What is more, a night a week for a month will return better dividends than crowding your study into a shorter period of time.
- Locate the place of the exam – You have been sent a notice telling you when and where to report for the examination. If the location is in a different town or otherwise unfamiliar to you, it would be well to inquire the best route and learn something about the building.
- Relax the night before the test – Allow your mind to rest. Do not study at all that night. Plan some mild recreation or diversion; then go to bed early and get a good night's sleep.
- Get up early enough to make a leisurely trip to the place for the test – This way unforeseen events, traffic snarls, unfamiliar buildings, etc. will not upset you.
- Dress comfortably – A written test is not a fashion show. You will be known by number and not by name, so wear something comfortable.

- Leave excess paraphernalia at home – Shopping bags and odd bundles will get in your way. You need bring only the items mentioned in the official notice you received; usually everything you need is provided. Do not bring reference books to the exam. They will only confuse those last minutes and be taken away from you when in the test room.
- Arrive somewhat ahead of time – If because of transportation schedules you must get there very early, bring a newspaper or magazine to take your mind off yourself while waiting.
- Locate the examination room – When you have found the proper room, you will be directed to the seat or part of the room where you will sit. Sometimes you are given a sheet of instructions to read while you are waiting. Do not fill out any forms until you are told to do so; just read them and be prepared.
- Relax and prepare to listen to the instructions
- If you have any physical problem that may keep you from doing your best, be sure to tell the test administrator. If you are sick or in poor health, you really cannot do your best on the exam. You can come back and take the test some other time.

VII. AT THE TEST

The day of the test is here and you have the test booklet in your hand. The temptation to get going is very strong. Caution! There is more to success than knowing the right answers. You must know how to identify your papers and understand variations in the type of short-answer question used in this particular examination. Follow these suggestions for maximum results from your efforts:

1) Cooperate with the monitor

The test administrator has a duty to create a situation in which you can be as much at ease as possible. He will give instructions, tell you when to begin, check to see that you are marking your answer sheet correctly, and so on. He is not there to guard you, although he will see that your competitors do not take unfair advantage. He wants to help you do your best.

2) Listen to all instructions

Don't jump the gun! Wait until you understand all directions. In most civil service tests you get more time than you need to answer the questions. So don't be in a hurry. Read each word of instructions until you clearly understand the meaning. Study the examples, listen to all announcements and follow directions. Ask questions if you do not understand what to do.

3) Identify your papers

Civil service exams are usually identified by number only. You will be assigned a number; you must not put your name on your test papers. Be sure to copy your number correctly. Since more than one exam may be given, copy your exact examination title.

4) Plan your time

Unless you are told that a test is a "speed" or "rate of work" test, speed itself is usually not important. Time enough to answer all the questions will be provided, but this does not mean that you have all day. An overall time limit has been set. Divide the total time (in minutes) by the number of questions to determine the approximate time you have for each question.

5) Do not linger over difficult questions

If you come across a difficult question, mark it with a paper clip (useful to have along) and come back to it when you have been through the booklet. One caution if you do this – be sure to skip a number on your answer sheet as well. Check often to be sure that you have not lost your place and that you are marking in the row numbered the same as the question you are answering.

6) Read the questions

Be sure you know what the question asks! Many capable people are unsuccessful because they failed to *read* the questions correctly.

7) Answer all questions

Unless you have been instructed that a penalty will be deducted for incorrect answers, it is better to guess than to omit a question.

8) Speed tests

It is often better NOT to guess on speed tests. It has been found that on timed tests people are tempted to spend the last few seconds before time is called in marking answers at random – without even reading them – in the hope of picking up a few extra points. To discourage this practice, the instructions may warn you that your score will be "corrected" for guessing. That is, a penalty will be applied. The incorrect answers will be deducted from the correct ones, or some other penalty formula will be used.

9) Review your answers

If you finish before time is called, go back to the questions you guessed or omitted to give them further thought. Review other answers if you have time.

10) Return your test materials

If you are ready to leave before others have finished or time is called, take ALL your materials to the monitor and leave quietly. Never take any test material with you. The monitor can discover whose papers are not complete, and taking a test booklet may be grounds for disqualification.

VIII. EXAMINATION TECHNIQUES

1) Read the general instructions carefully. These are usually printed on the first page of the exam booklet. As a rule, these instructions refer to the timing of the examination; the fact that you should not start work until the signal and must stop work at a signal, etc. If there are any *special* instructions, such as a choice of questions to be answered, make sure that you note this instruction carefully.

2) When you are ready to start work on the examination, that is as soon as the signal has been given, read the instructions to each question booklet, underline any key words or phrases, such as *least, best, outline, describe* and the like. In this way you will tend to answer as requested rather than discover on reviewing your paper that you *listed without describing*, that you selected the *worst* choice rather than the *best* choice, etc.

3) If the examination is of the objective or multiple-choice type – that is, each question will also give a series of possible answers: A, B, C or D, and you are called upon to select the best answer and write the letter next to that answer on your answer paper – it is advisable to start answering each question in turn. There may be anywhere from 50 to 100 such questions in the three or four hours allotted and you can see how much time would be taken if you read through all the questions before beginning to answer any. Furthermore, if you come across a question or group of questions which you know would be difficult to answer, it would undoubtedly affect your handling of all the other questions.

4) If the examination is of the essay type and contains but a few questions, it is a moot point as to whether you should read all the questions before starting to answer any one. Of course, if you are given a choice – say five out of seven and the like – then it is essential to read all the questions so you can eliminate the two that are most difficult. If, however, you are asked to answer all the questions, there may be danger in trying to answer the easiest one first because you may find that you will spend too much time on it. The best technique is to answer the first question, then proceed to the second, etc.

5) Time your answers. Before the exam begins, write down the time it started, then add the time allowed for the examination and write down the time it must be completed, then divide the time available somewhat as follows:
    - If 3-1/2 hours are allowed, that would be 210 minutes. If you have 80 objective-type questions, that would be an average of 2-1/2 minutes per question. Allow yourself no more than 2 minutes per question, or a total of 160 minutes, which will permit about 50 minutes to review.
    - If for the time allotment of 210 minutes there are 7 essay questions to answer, that would average about 30 minutes a question. Give yourself only 25 minutes per question so that you have about 35 minutes to review.

6) The most important instruction is to *read each question* and make sure you know what is wanted. The second most important instruction is to *time yourself properly* so that you answer every question. The third most important instruction is to *answer every question*. Guess if you have to but include something for each question. Remember that you will receive no credit for a blank and will probably receive some credit if you write something in answer to an essay question. If you guess a letter – say "B" for a multiple-choice question – you may have guessed right. If you leave a blank as an answer to a multiple-choice question, the examiners may respect your feelings but it will not add a point to your score. Some exams may penalize you for wrong answers, so in such cases *only*, you may not want to guess unless you have some basis for your answer.

7) Suggestions
    a. Objective-type questions
        1. Examine the question booklet for proper sequence of pages and questions
        2. Read all instructions carefully
        3. Skip any question which seems too difficult; return to it after all other questions have been answered
        4. Apportion your time properly; do not spend too much time on any single question or group of questions

5. Note and underline key words – *all, most, fewest, least, best, worst, same, opposite,* etc.
6. Pay particular attention to negatives
7. Note unusual option, e.g., unduly long, short, complex, different or similar in content to the body of the question
8. Observe the use of "hedging" words – *probably, may, most likely,* etc.
9. Make sure that your answer is put next to the same number as the question
10. Do not second-guess unless you have good reason to believe the second answer is definitely more correct
11. Cross out original answer if you decide another answer is more accurate; do not erase until you are ready to hand your paper in
12. Answer all questions; guess unless instructed otherwise
13. Leave time for review

  b. Essay questions
    1. Read each question carefully
    2. Determine exactly what is wanted. Underline key words or phrases.
    3. Decide on outline or paragraph answer
    4. Include many different points and elements unless asked to develop any one or two points or elements
    5. Show impartiality by giving pros and cons unless directed to select one side only
    6. Make and write down any assumptions you find necessary to answer the questions
    7. Watch your English, grammar, punctuation and choice of words
    8. Time your answers; don't crowd material

8) Answering the essay question

Most essay questions can be answered by framing the specific response around several key words or ideas. Here are a few such key words or ideas:

M's: manpower, materials, methods, money, management
P's: purpose, program, policy, plan, procedure, practice, problems, pitfalls, personnel, public relations

  a. Six basic steps in handling problems:
    1. Preliminary plan and background development
    2. Collect information, data and facts
    3. Analyze and interpret information, data and facts
    4. Analyze and develop solutions as well as make recommendations
    5. Prepare report and sell recommendations
    6. Install recommendations and follow up effectiveness

  b. Pitfalls to avoid
    1. *Taking things for granted* – A statement of the situation does not necessarily imply that each of the elements is necessarily true; for example, a complaint may be invalid and biased so that all that can be taken for granted is that a complaint has been registered

2. *Considering only one side of a situation* – Wherever possible, indicate several alternatives and then point out the reasons you selected the best one
3. *Failing to indicate follow up* – Whenever your answer indicates action on your part, make certain that you will take proper follow-up action to see how successful your recommendations, procedures or actions turn out to be
4. *Taking too long in answering any single question* – Remember to time your answers properly

IX. AFTER THE TEST

Scoring procedures differ in detail among civil service jurisdictions although the general principles are the same. Whether the papers are hand-scored or graded by machine we have described, they are nearly always graded by number. That is, the person who marks the paper knows only the number – never the name – of the applicant. Not until all the papers have been graded will they be matched with names. If other tests, such as training and experience or oral interview ratings have been given, scores will be combined. Different parts of the examination usually have different weights. For example, the written test might count 60 percent of the final grade, and a rating of training and experience 40 percent. In many jurisdictions, veterans will have a certain number of points added to their grades.

After the final grade has been determined, the names are placed in grade order and an eligible list is established. There are various methods for resolving ties between those who get the same final grade – probably the most common is to place first the name of the person whose application was received first. Job offers are made from the eligible list in the order the names appear on it. You will be notified of your grade and your rank as soon as all these computations have been made. This will be done as rapidly as possible.

People who are found to meet the requirements in the announcement are called "eligibles." Their names are put on a list of eligible candidates. An eligible's chances of getting a job depend on how high he stands on this list and how fast agencies are filling jobs from the list.

When a job is to be filled from a list of eligibles, the agency asks for the names of people on the list of eligibles for that job. When the civil service commission receives this request, it sends to the agency the names of the three people highest on this list. Or, if the job to be filled has specialized requirements, the office sends the agency the names of the top three persons who meet these requirements from the general list.

The appointing officer makes a choice from among the three people whose names were sent to him. If the selected person accepts the appointment, the names of the others are put back on the list to be considered for future openings.

That is the rule in hiring from all kinds of eligible lists, whether they are for typist, carpenter, chemist, or something else. For every vacancy, the appointing officer has his choice of any one of the top three eligibles on the list. This explains why the person whose name is on top of the list sometimes does not get an appointment when some of the persons lower on the list do. If the appointing officer chooses the second or third eligible, the No. 1 eligible does not get a job at once, but stays on the list until he is appointed or the list is terminated.

X. HOW TO PASS THE INTERVIEW TEST

The examination for which you applied requires an oral interview test. You have already taken the written test and you are now being called for the interview test – the final part of the formal examination.

You may think that it is not possible to prepare for an interview test and that there are no procedures to follow during an interview. Our purpose is to point out some things you can do in advance that will help you and some good rules to follow and pitfalls to avoid while you are being interviewed.

What is an interview supposed to test?

The written examination is designed to test the technical knowledge and competence of the candidate; the oral is designed to evaluate intangible qualities, not readily measured otherwise, and to establish a list showing the relative fitness of each candidate – as measured against his competitors – for the position sought. Scoring is not on the basis of "right" and "wrong," but on a sliding scale of values ranging from "not passable" to "outstanding." As a matter of fact, it is possible to achieve a relatively low score without a single "incorrect" answer because of evident weakness in the qualities being measured.

Occasionally, an examination may consist entirely of an oral test – either an individual or a group oral. In such cases, information is sought concerning the technical knowledges and abilities of the candidate, since there has been no written examination for this purpose. More commonly, however, an oral test is used to supplement a written examination.

Who conducts interviews?

The composition of oral boards varies among different jurisdictions. In nearly all, a representative of the personnel department serves as chairman. One of the members of the board may be a representative of the department in which the candidate would work. In some cases, "outside experts" are used, and, frequently, a businessman or some other representative of the general public is asked to serve. Labor and management or other special groups may be represented. The aim is to secure the services of experts in the appropriate field.

However the board is composed, it is a good idea (and not at all improper or unethical) to ascertain in advance of the interview who the members are and what groups they represent. When you are introduced to them, you will have some idea of their backgrounds and interests, and at least you will not stutter and stammer over their names.

What should be done before the interview?

While knowledge about the board members is useful and takes some of the surprise element out of the interview, there is other preparation which is more substantive. It *is* possible to prepare for an oral interview – in several ways:

1) Keep a copy of your application and review it carefully before the interview

This may be the only document before the oral board, and the starting point of the interview. Know what education and experience you have listed there, and the sequence and dates of all of it. Sometimes the board will ask you to review the highlights of your experience for them; you should not have to hem and haw doing it.

2) Study the class specification and the examination announcement

Usually, the oral board has one or both of these to guide them. The qualities, characteristics or knowledges required by the position sought are stated in these documents. They offer valuable clues as to the nature of the oral interview. For example, if the job involves supervisory responsibilities, the announcement will usually indicate that knowledge of modern supervisory methods and the qualifications of the candidate as a supervisor will be tested. If so, you can expect such questions, frequently in the form of a hypothetical situation which you are expected to solve. NEVER go into an oral without knowledge of the duties and responsibilities of the job you seek.

3) Think through each qualification required

Try to visualize the kind of questions you would ask if you were a board member. How well could you answer them? Try especially to appraise your own knowledge and background in each area, *measured against the job sought*, and identify any areas in which you are weak. Be critical and realistic – do not flatter yourself.

4) Do some general reading in areas in which you feel you may be weak

For example, if the job involves supervision and your past experience has NOT, some general reading in supervisory methods and practices, particularly in the field of human relations, might be useful. Do NOT study agency procedures or detailed manuals. The oral board will be testing your understanding and capacity, not your memory.

5) Get a good night's sleep and watch your general health and mental attitude

You will want a clear head at the interview. Take care of a cold or any other minor ailment, and of course, no hangovers.

What should be done on the day of the interview?

Now comes the day of the interview itself. Give yourself plenty of time to get there. Plan to arrive somewhat ahead of the scheduled time, particularly if your appointment is in the fore part of the day. If a previous candidate fails to appear, the board might be ready for you a bit early. By early afternoon an oral board is almost invariably behind schedule if there are many candidates, and you may have to wait. Take along a book or magazine to read, or your application to review, but leave any extraneous material in the waiting room when you go in for your interview. In any event, relax and compose yourself.

The matter of dress is important. The board is forming impressions about you – from your experience, your manners, your attitude, and your appearance. Give your personal appearance careful attention. Dress your best, but not your flashiest. Choose conservative, appropriate clothing, and be sure it is immaculate. This is a business interview, and your appearance should indicate that you regard it as such. Besides, being well groomed and properly dressed will help boost your confidence.

Sooner or later, someone will call your name and escort you into the interview room. *This is it.* From here on you are on your own. It is too late for any more preparation. But remember, you asked for this opportunity to prove your fitness, and you are here because your request was granted.

What happens when you go in?

The usual sequence of events will be as follows: The clerk (who is often the board stenographer) will introduce you to the chairman of the oral board, who will introduce you to the other members of the board. Acknowledge the introductions before you sit down. Do not be surprised if you find a microphone facing you or a stenotypist sitting by. Oral interviews are usually recorded in the event of an appeal or other review.

Usually the chairman of the board will open the interview by reviewing the highlights of your education and work experience from your application – primarily for the benefit of the other members of the board, as well as to get the material into the record. Do not interrupt or comment unless there is an error or significant misinterpretation; if that is the case, do not hesitate. But do not quibble about insignificant matters. Also, he will usually ask you some question about your education, experience or your present job – partly to get you to start talking and to establish the interviewing "rapport." He may start the actual questioning, or turn it over to one of the other members. Frequently, each member undertakes the questioning on a particular area, one in which he is perhaps most competent, so you can expect each member to participate in the examination. Because time is limited, you may also expect some rather abrupt switches in the direction the questioning takes, so do not be upset by it. Normally, a board member will not pursue a single line of questioning unless he discovers a particular strength or weakness.

After each member has participated, the chairman will usually ask whether any member has any further questions, then will ask you if you have anything you wish to add. Unless you are expecting this question, it may floor you. Worse, it may start you off on an extended, extemporaneous speech. The board is not usually seeking more information. The question is principally to offer you a last opportunity to present further qualifications or to indicate that you have nothing to add. So, if you feel that a significant qualification or characteristic has been overlooked, it is proper to point it out in a sentence or so. Do not compliment the board on the thoroughness of their examination – they have been sketchy, and you know it. If you wish, merely say, "No thank you, I have nothing further to add." This is a point where you can "talk yourself out" of a good impression or fail to present an important bit of information. Remember, *you close the interview yourself*.

The chairman will then say, "That is all, Mr. _____, thank you." Do not be startled; the interview is over, and quicker than you think. Thank him, gather your belongings and take your leave. Save your sigh of relief for the other side of the door.

How to put your best foot forward

Throughout this entire process, you may feel that the board individually and collectively is trying to pierce your defenses, seek out your hidden weaknesses and embarrass and confuse you. Actually, this is not true. They are obliged to make an appraisal of your qualifications for the job you are seeking, and they want to see you in your best light. Remember, they must interview all candidates and a non-cooperative candidate may become a failure in spite of their best efforts to bring out his qualifications. Here are 15 suggestions that will help you:

1) Be natural – Keep your attitude confident, not cocky

If you are not confident that you can do the job, do not expect the board to be. Do not apologize for your weaknesses, try to bring out your strong points. The board is interested in a positive, not negative, presentation. Cockiness will antagonize any board member and make him wonder if you are covering up a weakness by a false show of strength.

2) Get comfortable, but don't lounge or sprawl

Sit erectly but not stiffly. A careless posture may lead the board to conclude that you are careless in other things, or at least that you are not impressed by the importance of the occasion. Either conclusion is natural, even if incorrect. Do not fuss with your clothing, a pencil or an ashtray. Your hands may occasionally be useful to emphasize a point; do not let them become a point of distraction.

3) Do not wisecrack or make small talk

This is a serious situation, and your attitude should show that you consider it as such. Further, the time of the board is limited – they do not want to waste it, and neither should you.

4) Do not exaggerate your experience or abilities

In the first place, from information in the application or other interviews and sources, the board may know more about you than you think. Secondly, you probably will not get away with it. An experienced board is rather adept at spotting such a situation, so do not take the chance.

5) If you know a board member, do not make a point of it, yet do not hide it

Certainly you are not fooling him, and probably not the other members of the board. Do not try to take advantage of your acquaintanceship – it will probably do you little good.

6) Do not dominate the interview

Let the board do that. They will give you the clues – do not assume that you have to do all the talking. Realize that the board has a number of questions to ask you, and do not try to take up all the interview time by showing off your extensive knowledge of the answer to the first one.

7) Be attentive

You only have 20 minutes or so, and you should keep your attention at its sharpest throughout. When a member is addressing a problem or question to you, give him your undivided attention. Address your reply principally to him, but do not exclude the other board members.

8) Do not interrupt

A board member may be stating a problem for you to analyze. He will ask you a question when the time comes. Let him state the problem, and wait for the question.

9) Make sure you understand the question

Do not try to answer until you are sure what the question is. If it is not clear, restate it in your own words or ask the board member to clarify it for you. However, do not haggle about minor elements.

10) Reply promptly but not hastily

A common entry on oral board rating sheets is "candidate responded readily," or "candidate hesitated in replies." Respond as promptly and quickly as you can, but do not jump to a hasty, ill-considered answer.

11) Do not be peremptory in your answers

A brief answer is proper – but do not fire your answer back. That is a losing game from your point of view. The board member can probably ask questions much faster than you can answer them.

12) Do not try to create the answer you think the board member wants

He is interested in what kind of mind you have and how it works – not in playing games. Furthermore, he can usually spot this practice and will actually grade you down on it.

13) Do not switch sides in your reply merely to agree with a board member

Frequently, a member will take a contrary position merely to draw you out and to see if you are willing and able to defend your point of view. Do not start a debate, yet do not surrender a good position. If a position is worth taking, it is worth defending.

14) Do not be afraid to admit an error in judgment if you are shown to be wrong

The board knows that you are forced to reply without any opportunity for careful consideration. Your answer may be demonstrably wrong. If so, admit it and get on with the interview.

15) Do not dwell at length on your present job

The opening question may relate to your present assignment. Answer the question but do not go into an extended discussion. You are being examined for a *new* job, not your present one. As a matter of fact, try to phrase ALL your answers in terms of the job for which you are being examined.

Basis of Rating

Probably you will forget most of these "do's" and "don'ts" when you walk into the oral interview room. Even remembering them all will not ensure you a passing grade. Perhaps you did not have the qualifications in the first place. But remembering them will help you to put your best foot forward, without treading on the toes of the board members.

Rumor and popular opinion to the contrary notwithstanding, an oral board wants you to make the best appearance possible. They know you are under pressure – but they also want to see how you respond to it as a guide to what your reaction would be under the pressures of the job you seek. They will be influenced by the degree of poise you display, the personal traits you show and the manner in which you respond.

ABOUT THIS BOOK

This book contains tests divided into Examination Sections. Go through each test, answering every question in the margin. We have also attached a sample answer sheet at the back of the book that can be removed and used. At the end of each test look at the answer key and check your answers. On the ones you got wrong, look at the right answer choice and learn. Do not fill in the answers first. Do not memorize the questions and answers, but understand the answer and principles involved. On your test, the questions will likely be different from the samples. Questions are changed and new ones added. If you understand these past questions you should have success with any changes that arise. Tests may consist of several types of questions. We have additional books on each subject should more study be advisable or necessary for you. Finally, the more you study, the better prepared you will be. This book is intended to be the last thing you study before you walk into the examination room. Prior study of relevant texts is also recommended. NLC publishes some of these in our Fundamental Series. Knowledge and good sense are important factors in passing your exam. Good luck also helps. So now study this Passbook, absorb the material contained within and take that knowledge into the examination. Then do your best to pass that exam.

EXAMINATION SECTION

EXAMINATION SECTION
TEST 1

DIRECTIONS: Each question or incomplete statement is followed by several suggested answers or completions. Select the one that BEST answers the question or completes the statement. *PRINT THE LETTER OF THE CORRECT ANSWER IN THE SPACE AT THE RIGHT.*

Questions 1-16.

DIRECTIONS: Questions 1 through 16 deal with graphical symbols of electrical items as recommended by the ANSI (ex-ASA). For each item, select the proper graphical symbol and print the letter corresponding to it.

1. Telephone switchboard

    A. 6   B. 16   C. 17   D. 18

2. Exit light wall outlet

    A. 5   B. 12   C. 15   D. 16

3. City fire alarm station

    A. 19   B. 21   C. 22   D. 23

4. Electric door opener

    A. 9   B. 10   C. 11   D. 15

5. Duplex convenience outlet

    A. 9   B. 10   C. 15   D. 24

6. Range outlet

    A. 3   B. 6   C. 13   D. 14

7. Push button

    A. 5   B. 8   C. 11   D. 12

8. Power panel

    A. 1   B. 2   C. 3   D. 4

1.____

2.____

3.____

4.____

5.____

6.____

7.____

8.____

2 (#1)

9. Four-way switch

    A. 4   B. 13   C. 14   D. 16

10. Controller

    A. 3   B. 4   C. 5   D. 9

11. Lighting panel

    A. 1   B. 2   C. 3   D. 4

12. Buzzer

    A. 3   B. 5   C. 8   D. 11

13. Isolating switch

    A. 3   B. 5   C. 9   D. 10

14. Interconnecting telephone

    A. 13   B. 14   C. 17   D. 18

15. Fire alarm central station

    A. 21   B. 22   C. 23   D. 26

16. Clock outlet

    A. 9   B. 10   C. 15   D. 26

18. [horn symbol]

19. S_F

20. S_{MC}

21. [FA]

22. [F]

23. [envelope symbol]

24. [single-tube fixture symbol]

25. [three-tube fixture symbol] 3

26. Ⓒ

9. ____

10. ____

11. ____

12. ____

13. ____

14. ____

15. ____

16. ____

17. A riser diagram is an electrical drawing which would give information about the

    A. voltage drop in feeders
    B. size of feeders and panel loads
    C. external connections to equipment
    D. sequence of operation of devices and equipment

18. When a contractor fails to adhere to an approved progress schedule, he should

    A. revise the schedule without delay
    B. ask for an extension of time on account of delays
    C. adopt such additional means and methods of construction as will make up for the time lost
    D. take no immediate action with the hope that sufficient time will be available later on that will assure the completion in accordance with the schedule

19. The usual contract for work includes a section entitled, *Instructions to Bidders,* which states that the

    A. contractor agrees that he has made his own examination and will make no claims for damages on account of errors or omissions
    B. contractor shall not make claims for damages of any discrepancy, error or omission in any plans
    C. estimates of quantities and calculations are guaranteed by the Board to be correct and are deemed to be a representation of the conditions affecting the work
    D. plans, measurements, dimensions, and conditions under which the work is to be performed are guaranteed by the Board

20. The purpose of performing a dielectric test on a sample of oil taken from the casing of an oil-filled power transformer is to determine the

    A. viscosity
    B. insulating quality
    C. flashpoint
    D. extent of contamination

21. A neon test lamp can be used to test

    A. the field intensity of a relay magnet
    B. the phase rotation of a source of supply
    C. whether a supply source is A.C. or D.C.
    D. the power factor of a source of supply

22. The size, in circular mils, of a wire whose diameter is known can be calculated by

    A. multiplying the diameter in mils by $\pi/4$
    B. squaring the diameter in mils
    C. squaring the diameter in mils and multiplying the product by $\pi/4$
    D. squaring the diameter in inches

23. The short time rating and the continuous rating of a given piece of electrical machinery differ, but both are based on the

    A. cost of energy
    B. line potential

C. power factor of the machine
D. temperature rise of the machine

24. A lump sum type of contract may require the contractor to submit a schedule of unit prices. 24._____
The BEST reason for this is that it

   A. prevents the lump sum from being too high
   B. simplifies the selection of the lowest bidder
   C. enables the estimators to check the total cost
   D. provides a means of making equitable partial payments

25. In assigning his men to various jobs, the BEST principle for a supervisor to follow is to 25._____

   A. study the men's abilities and assign them accordingly
   B. rotate a man from job to job until you find one which he can do well
   C. assign each of them a job and let them adjust to it in their own way
   D. assume that men appointed to the position can do all parts of the work equally wel

---

KEY (CORRECT ANSWERS)

1. D		11. A	
2. B		12. B	
3. D		13. A	
4. B		14. C	
5. D		15. A	
6. C		16. D	
7. B		17. B	
8. B		18. C	
9. D		19. A	
10. B		20. C	

21. C
22. B
23. D
24. D
25. A

TEST 2

DIRECTIONS: Each question or incomplete statement is followed by several suggested answers or completions. Select the one that BEST answers the question or completes the statement. *PRINT THE LETTER OF THE CORRECT ANSWER IN THE SPACE AT THE RIGHT.*

Questions 1-8.

DIRECTIONS: Questions 1 through 8 are to be answered in accordance with the requirements of the electrical code, assuming normal procedures. Do NOT consider exceptions which are granted by special permission.

1. The MINIMUM size of A.W.G. wire which may be used on a 15-ampere branch circuit is 1.____

   A. 10   B. 12   C. 14   D. 16

2. Conductors supplying an individual motor whose full-load current is 100 amperes should have a MINIMUM carrying capacity of _____ amperes. 2.____

   A. 100   B. 115   C. 125   D. 150

3. The MINIMUM rating of a service switch is _____ amperes. 3.____

   A. 30   B. 60   C. 100   D. 200

4. In the installation of fluorescent fixtures, the MAXIMUM number of single or two-lamp type auxiliaries which can be placed on any single fifteen-ampere branch circuit is 4.____

   A. 10   B. 12   C. 15   D. 18

5. Where rubber-covered conductors are used in a conduit, the MINIMUM radius of the curve of the inner edge of any field bend, in terms of the internal diameter of the conduit, shall not be less than _____ times. 5.____

   A. 4   B. 6   C. 8   D. 10

6. Except for fixture wire of MI cable, single conductors of No. 6 A.W.G. or smaller intended for use as identified conductors of circuits shall have an outer identification of 6.____

   A. green
   B. black
   C. white or natural gray
   D. gray with a yellow marker throughout its length

7. Motor running protective devices, other than fuses, should have a continuous current-carrying capacity, in terms of the full load current rating of the motor, of AT LEAST 7.____

   A. 100%   B. 115%   C. 120%   D. 125%

8. The one of the following which should ALWAYS be used as the grounding electrode, where available, is a 8.____

   A. driven non-ferrous metallic rod
   B. buried plate with an area of 2 sq.ft.
   C. driven iron rod with a resistance of 25 ohms
   D. continuous metallic underground water piping system

5

9. The MAIN reason for requiring written job reports is to 9.____

   A. avoid the necessity of oral orders
   B. develop better methods of doing the work
   C. provide a permanent record of what was done
   D. increase the amount of work that can be done

10. Of the following items, the one which should NOT be included in a proposed work sched- 10.____
    ule is

    A. a schedule of hourly wage rates and supplementary benefits
    B. an estimated time required for delivery of materials and equipment
    C. the anticipated commencement and completion of the various operations
    D. the sequence and inter-relationship of various operations with those of related contracts

11. The closed circuit is used primarily in communication and fire alarm systems to indicate, 11.____
    by various or audible means, which of the following abnormal circuit conditions?

    A. Open   B. Ground
    C. Overload   D. Direct short

12. A Board specification states that access panels to suspended ceiling will be of metal. 12.____
    The MAIN reason for providing access panels is to

    A. improve the insulation of the ceiling
    B. improve the appearance of the building
    C. make it easier to construct the building
    D. make it easier to maintain the building

13. The one of the following which is a successful means of decreasing electrolysis in 13.____
    underground metal pipes is to

    A. use galvanized pipe
    B. insert occasional insulating joints in the pipes
    C. keep the voltage drop in the ground return circuit over 15 volts
    D. coat the pipe with tar for 6 inches above and 6 inches below the point where it
       enters the ground

14. The abbreviation *MCM* placed next to a feeder cable in a wiring diagram would indicate 14.____
    the

    A. microamperes per circular mil
    B. area of the cable in millions of circular mils
    C. area of the cable in thousands of circular mils
    D. resistance of the cable in microhms per circular-mil-ft.

15. Which one of the following is the PRIMARY object in drawing up a set of specifications 15.____
    for materials to be purchased?

    A. Control of quality
    B. Outline of intended use
    C. Establishment of standard sizes
    D. Location and method of inspection

16. The marking or lettering that indicates a conductor having moisture-and-heat resistance thermoplastic covering and which may be used in both dry and wet locations is

    A. RHW B. SB C. THW D. TW

17. In performing field inspectional work, an inspector is the contact man between the public and the authority, and it is his job to secure compliance through the maximum utilization of persuasion and education and the minimum application of coercion.
    According to the above statement, an inspector performing inspectional duties should

    A. seek to obtain voluntary compliance and use coercion only as a last resort
    B. be conciliatory on all issues of non-compliance and not take an attitude of firmness and authority
    C. maintain a strictly impersonal attitude in the exercise of his duties at all times
    D. use the threat of legal action to secure conformance with specified requirements

18. In a polarized interior lighting system, the

    A. base of the lamp sockets is connected to the identified wire
    B. branch circuit light switch is connected to the identifying wire
    C. screwshells of the lamp sockets are connected to the identified wire
    D. branch circuit light switch is connected to the screwshell of the lamp socket

19. If a supervisor finds a discrepancy between the plans and specifications, he should

    A. always follow the plans
    B. ask for an interpretation
    C. always follow the specifications
    D. follow the plans if the difference is in dimensions

20. The BEST way to evaluate the overall state of completion of a construction project is to check the progress estimate against the

    A. inspection work sheet
    B. construction schedule
    C. inspector's checklist
    D. equipment maintenance schedule

21. Two-phase power may be converted to 3-phase power, or vice versa, by using which of the following transformer connections?

    A. Scott   B. Delta-wye
    C. Open delta   D. Autotransformer

22. The CHIEF purpose in preparing an outline for a report is usually to insure that

    A. the report will be grammatically correct
    B. every point will be given equal emphasis
    C. principal and secondary points will be properly integrated
    D. the language of the report will be of the same level and include the same technical terms

23. A contractor on a large construction project USUALLY receives partial payments based on

    A. estimates of completed work
    B. actual cost of materials delivered and work completed
    C. estimates of material delivered and not paid for by the contractor
    D. the breakdown estimate submitted after the contract was signed and prorated over the estimated duration of the contract

23.____

24. In testing insulation resistance, the MAIN reason that the use of a megger is *preferable* to the use of an ordinary ohmmeter is that a megger

    A. is more rugged
    B. does not require constant care
    C. has a lower internal resistance
    D. usually operates at the proper voltage

24.____

25. In order to avoid disputes over payments for extra work in a contract for construction, the BEST procedure to follow would be to

    A. have contractor submit work progress reports daily
    B. insert a special clause in the contract specifications
    C. have a representative on the job at all times to verify conditions
    D. allocate a certain percentage of the cost of the job to cover such expenses

25.____

KEY (CORRECT ANSWERS)

1.	B		11.	A
2.	C		12.	D
3.	C		13.	B
4.	C		14.	C
5.	B		15.	A
6.	C		16.	C
7.	B		17.	A
8.	D		18.	C
9.	C		19.	B
10.	A		20.	B

21. A
22. C
23. A
24. D
25. C

TEST 3

DIRECTIONS: Each question or incomplete statement is followed by several suggested answers or completions. Select the one that BEST answers the question or completes the statement. *PRINT THE LETTER OF THE CORRECT ANSWER IN THE SPACE AT THE RIGHT.*

1. During the actual construction work, the CHIEF value of a construction schedule is to   1.____

    A. insure that the work will be done on time
    B. reveal whether production is falling behind
    C. show how much equipment and material is required for the project
    D. furnish data as to the methods and techniques of construction operations

2. Prior to the installation of equipment called for in the specifications, the contractor is usually required to submit for approval   2.____

    A. sets of shop drawings
    B. a set of revised specifications
    C. a detailed description of the methods of work to be used
    D. a complete list of skilled and unskilled tradesmen he proposes to use

3. An inspector inspecting a large building under construction inspected lighting fixtures at 9 A.M. and electrical feeders at 10 A.M., machine connections at 11 A.M., and did his office work in the afternoon. He followed the same pattern daily for months.
   This procedure is   3.____

    A. *bad*, because not enough time is devoted to important electrical feeders
    B. *bad*, because the tradesmen know when the inspections occur
    C. *good*, because it is methodical and he does not miss any of the trades
    D. *good*, because it gives equal amount of time to the important trades

4. A rule of thumb for calculating the area of copper conductors in C.M. as given in the AWG tables is that for every _____ size, the wire cross section _____.   4.____

    A. second gage of larger; doubles
    B. second gage of larger; increases four times
    C. third gage of smaller; is halved
    D. third gage of smaller; is one-third

5. The drawing which should be used as a legal reference when checking completed construction work is the _____ drawing(s).   5.____

    A. contract   B. assembly
    C. working or shop   D. preliminary

6. The motor starting device commonly called a compensator is actually a(n)   6.____

    A. rheostat   B. potentiometer
    C. auto-transformer   D. capacitor

7. The BEST way for a supervisor to determine whether a new employee is learning his work properly is to   7.____

A. ask the other men how this man is making out
B. question him directly on details of the work
C. assume that if he asks no questions he knows the work
D. inspect and follow up on the work which is assigned to him

Questions 8-13.

DIRECTIONS: Questions 8 through 13 refer to the circuit drawn below.

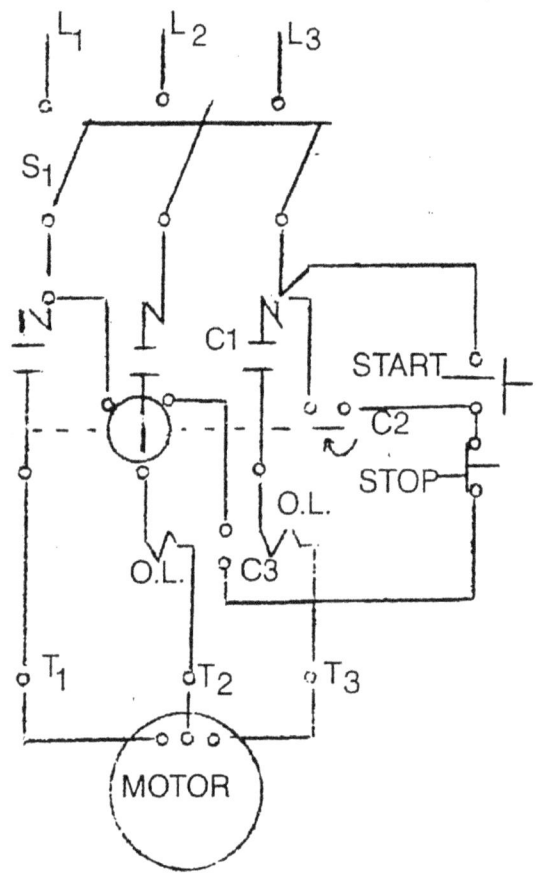

8. The circuitry shown is called a(n)

    A. D.C. motor controller
    B. reduced voltage starter
    C. two-speed motor control
    D. across-the-line starter

9. The circuit element indicated by C_1 is a

    A. capacitor
    B. circuit breaker
    C. pair of contacts which is normally open
    D. pair of start button contacts

10. If the motor is of the three-phase induction type, the incoming power is MOST likely   10.____

    A. plus and minus 115 volts D.C.
    B. 115 volts A.C. with neutral
    C. 208 volts A.C. line-to-line
    D. 230 volts D.C. with neutral

11. The PROPER designation for line switch S_1 is   11.____

    A. SPST   B. 3PDT   C. 3TSP   D. 3TDP

12. The O.L. relays are in the circuitry to   12.____

    A. protect the motor from overvoltages
    B. keep the stop button in after it has been depressed
    C. allow the motor to be operated on two lines if desired
    D. interrupt the contactor holding circuit on sustained overloads

13. The purpose of contact C_2 is to   13.____

    A. hold the start button in after it has been depressed
    B. hold the contactor in when the line voltages drop too low
    C. hold the contactor in after the start button has been depressed
    D. de-energize the contactor solenoid when the stop button is depressed

14. One ADVANTAGE of fluorescent lamps over incandescent lamps is that they   14.____

    A. are easier to handle
    B. are more efficient
    C. have simpler wiring circuits
    D. are not affected by temperature changes

15. To control a light fixture from three different locations, it is necessary to use _____ switches.   15.____

    A. one 4-way and two 3-way   B. three 3-way
    C. three 2-way   D. three single-pole

16. Good inspection methods require that the inspector   16.____

    A. be observant and check all details
    B. constantly check with the engineer who designed the school
    C. apply specifications according to his interpretations
    D. permit slight job violations to establish good public relations

17. Assume you are recommending in a report to your superior that a radical change in a standard maintenance procedure should be adopted.   17.____
    Of the following, the MOST important information to be included in this report is

    A. a list of the reasons for making this change
    B. the names of the other supervisors who favor the change
    C. a complete description of the present procedure
    D. amount of training time needed for the new procedure

18. A fixed amount of money is generally withheld from the contractor for a definite period after the completion of construction.
    The BEST reason for this is

    A. that the money will be available for taxes due
    B. to penalize the contractor for poor work
    C. that it is a security for the repair of any defective work
    D. that the money will be available for modifications in the design of the structure

18.____

19. The frequency with which job reports are submitted should depend MAINLY on

    A. how comprehensive the report has to be
    B. the amount of information in the report
    C. the availability of an experienced man to write the report
    D. the importance of changes in the information included in the report

19.____

20. The use of groups of combinations of conductors in the same conduit will

    A. decrease conductor resistance
    B. be allowed for circuit voltages not exceeding 250V
    C. upgrade the current-carrying capacity of the conductors
    D. downgrade the current-carrying capacity of the conductors

20.____

KEY (CORRECT ANSWERS)

1.	B	11.	A
2.	A	12.	D
3.	B	13.	C
4.	C	14.	B
5.	A	15.	A
6.	C	16.	A
7.	B	17.	A
8.	D	18.	C
9.	C	19.	D
10.	C	20.	D

EXAMINATION SECTION
TEST 1

DIRECTIONS: Each question or incomplete statement is followed by several suggested answers or completions. Select the one that BEST answers the question or completes the statement. *PRINT THE LETTER OF THE CORRECT ANSWER IN THE SPACE AT THE RIGHT.*

1. The MINIMUM number of appliance branch circuits required in the area comprising the kitchen, pantry, breakfast room, or dining alcove of dwelling occupancies is 1._____

    A. 1 B. 2 C. 3 D. 4

2. In a living room, at least one receptacle outlet shall be provided *every* _____ feet. 2._____

    A. 15 B. 12 C. 10 D. 6

3. Assume that new forty-watt fluorescent fixture ballasts which are not of the simple reactance type are being installed. 3._____
   According to code regulations governing fluorescent fixture ballast protection, these fixture ballasts

    A. cannot use non-renewable, non-resetting thermal protectors
    B. must be thermally protected
    C. can be protected by external exposed thermal protection
    D. cannot use (thermostatic) automatic resetting thermal protectors

4. According to the code regulations on grounding of electrical systems, the neutral of a 4-wire, 3-phase A.C. system in an office building 4._____

    A. is grounded at the service entrance
    B. need not be grounded
    C. must be tied to the conduit system at each panel board
    D. is connected at each motor to a green grounding conductor

5. With regard to the grounding of electrical systems, it is CORRECT to state that electrical systems 5._____

    A. must always be grounded
    B. must be provided with a ground detector, if ungrounded
    C. must always have a separate grounding conductor
    D. of less than fifty volts need not be grounded

6. With regard to the position or arrangement of the disconnecting means of a motor, it is CORRECT to say that the disconnecting equipment 6._____

    A. must always be within the line of sight
    B. are always in the same enclosure as the motor controller
    C. must be on the motor frame
    D. can be arranged to be locked in the open position

13

7. A 60-ampere subfeeder is connected to a 300-ampere main feeder. In order to properly protect the subfeeder,

   A. the protective device must be installed within one foot of the tap
   B. the protective device must be within five feet of the tap
   C. only fuses may be used
   D. only circuit breakers may be used

8. Assume that a three-phase feeder with its neutral is in a raceway. The *allowable* current capacity of the cable is _____ the appropriate tables in the code.

   A. greater than that obtained from
   B. 90 percent less than that obtained from
   C. the same as that obtained from
   D. 80 percent less than shown in

9. For rewiring existing raceways, the number of conductors permitted is _____ for new raceways.

   A. greater than
   B. the same as
   C. less than
   D. sixty-five percent greater than

10. The current capacity of copper bars is determined by using

    A. appropriate tables
    B. a current density of 100 amperes per sq. inch
    C. a current density of 500 amperes per sq. inch
    D. calculated short circuit forces

11. A special junction box is to be ordered to meet an unusual situation. The size of the box is determined PRIMARILY by the

    A. space available in which to locate the box
    B. location of the box
    C. material of which the box is made
    D. number and size of the wires running through or terminating in the box

12. When it is necessary to install three sets of parallel service feeders, the code requires that

    A. the conductors of each phase should be run in the same conduit
    B. the neutrals should be run in one conduit
    C. the conductors of each phase can be of greatly different lengths
    D. each phase conductor and the neutral conductor, if used, must be installed in each conduit

13. In order to pull a four-wire 250,000 cm RHW feeder into a conduit through a property line junction box, the type of lubricant that should be used is

    A. a heavy oil   B. graphite or talc
    C. a light oil   D. a light automotive grease

14. A 4"-conduit run changes its direction from horizontal to vertical and a pull box is installed at this point to facilitate fishing wire into the conduit.
For this purpose, it is BEST to place

    A. an elbow at the turn and install the box close by in the straight run of conduit
    B. the box at the turn, with the largest dimension in the horizontal direction
    C. the box at the turn, with the largest dimension in the vertical direction
    D. the box at the turn with the largest dimension at right angles to both the vertical and the horizontal conduits

15. The BEST way to attach a wire to a screw terminal is to

    A. place it straight under the screw head
    B. form a counterclockwise loop under the screw head
    C. form a clockwise loop under the screw head
    D. place the straight wire under the right side of the screw head

16. The MINIMUM number of wattmeters which may be used to measure the power in a delta-connected unbalanced three-phase load is

    A. 1   B. 2   C. 3   D. 4

17. An open-circuit test on a transformer is used to measure

    A. core losses
    B. copper losses
    C. windage and friction losses
    D. full-load efficiency

18. A meter that is used to measure the total energy consumed is a(n)

    A. demand meter   B. watt-hour meter
    C. ampere-hour meter   D. wattmeter

19. Assume that you are given a group of resistors with values ranging from 5 ohms to 10 megohms.
Of the following types of equipment, the one that you would use to sort them out is a(n)

    A. continuity checker made up of a battery and buzzer
    B. test lamp
    C. low-resistance voltmeter and battery
    D. ohmmeter

20. A 20:1 potential transformer is used to measure the voltage of a high voltage line.
If a voltmeter on the secondary of the transformer indicates 180 volts, the line voltage is MOST NEARLY _____ volts.

    A. 9   B. 360   C. 3600   D. 4000

21. A 50:1 current transformer in a feeder line has a 0-1 ammeter connected to its secondary.
If the meter indicates 0.5 amperes, the line current is MOST NEARLY _____ amperes.

    A. 0.01   B. 0.1   C. 2.5   D. 25

22. After a wiring installation is completed and it is found to be free of shorts and grounds, it *still* must be tested for

   A. dielectric strength
   B. arc-over voltage
   C. breakdown voltage
   D. insulation resistance

23. A voltmeter has a resistance of 1000 ohms on its 1-volt range. Its 250-volt range will have a resistance of MOST NEARLY _____ ohms.

   A. 250,000   B. 249,000   C. 25,000   D. 24,900

24. A voltmeter is marked 10,000 ohms per volt. It is used on its 150-volt range to measure a 100-volt source. The resistance of the voltmeter on this range is MOST NEARLY _____ ohms.

   A. 10,000   B. 100,000   C. 1,000,000   D. 1,500,000

25. A short-circuit test on a transformer is used to measure

   A. core losses
   B. copper losses
   C. stray power losses
   D. full load efficiency

KEY (CORRECT ANSWERS)

1. B	11. D
2. A	12. D
3. B	13. B
4. A	14. A
5. D	15. C
6. D	16. B
7. B	17. A
8. C	18. B
9. A	19. D
10. A	20. C

21. D
22. D
23. A
24. D
25. B

TEST 2

DIRECTIONS: Each question or incomplete statement is followed by several suggested answers or completions. Select the one that BEST answers the question or completes the statement. *PRINT THE LETTER OF THE CORRECT ANSWER IN THE SPACE AT THE RIGHT.*

1. The symbol S_4 on a plan indicates

   A. a four-way switch
   B. four switches
   C. signal number 4
   D. a switch for circuit number 4

   1.____

2. The symbol ⊖ on a plan stands for a

   A. single convenience outlet
   B. duplex convenience outlet
   C. male plug
   D. ceiling outlet

   2.____

3. A floor plan of light and power wiring is a

   A. detailed schematic showing the interconnection of all wiring involved
   B. detailed schematic showing color coding of all wiring interconnections for a given floor
   C. single line drawing showing wiring runs and the location of all outlets and runs for a given floor
   D. detailed layout of conduit runs showing all boxes and conduit connections for a given floor

   3.____

4. In order to determine from electrical plans the quantity of a particular size of conduit to be ordered,

   A. the distance of all runs of that particular size should be totaled
   B. the distance of all runs of that particular size should be totaled and increased by 5%
   C. no allowance should be made for vertical runs of that particular size
   D. count the number of boxes and multiply by an empirical factor for that particular size, obtained from experience

   4.____

5. Specifications for a store-and-office building specify a 2000-watt sign outlet over the entrance to each store, but nothing is indicated on the plans.
   This means that

   A. the outlet must be installed by the contractor
   B. the outlet need not be installed
   C. an extra charge will be allowed for installing the outlet
   D. no additional switches or circuit breakers need be provided

   5.____

6. Assume that, in a certain contract, the plans as approved by the bureau of gas and electricity show number 10 AWG wires rated at 30 amperes supplying 16-ampere loads protected by 20-ampere circuit breakers.
The PROPER action to be taken by contractor is that he

   A. can add additional loads up to 20 amperes
   B. can change the breakers to 30 amperes and increase the loads to 24 amperes
   C. must install the wiring in accordance with the plans
   D. can tell the owner that he can save him money by increasing the loads per circuit and reducing the number of circuits

7. The symbol shown at the right on a solenoid-controlled motor starting schematic indicates a
   A. variable capacitor and a fuse
   B. normally closed contact and a fuse
   C. normally closed contact and a circuit breaker
   D. thermal overload relay

8. A standard three-phase 208V motor contactor controls a pump motor for a water tower.
In MOST common installations of this type, the float switch

   A. has contacts through which the motor current flows
   B. operates the contactor solenoid
   C. operates a relay which in turn operates the motor control solenoid
   D. controls a solid state switch

9. Plans show two multiple feeders each of 250 MCM size.
The contractor proposes to install one set of 500 MCM size and claims that ample capacity is thereby obtained.
As an inspector, you should

   A. not permit the installation
   B. permit the installation without further consultation
   C. permit the installation but write a report to your supervisor
   D. tell the contractor to obtain approval from the code revision and interpretation committee

10. The pushbutton control for a 10 HP motor USUALLY is a(n)

    A. on-off switch
    B. single-pole double-throw switch
    C. double-pole double-throw switch
    D. momentary-contact switch in series with a normally closed spring-loaded switch

11. The president of a tenant's association calls the bureau of gas and electricity and complains about dangerous open wiring. You are assigned to investigate this complaint.
The BEST procedure for you to follow is to

    A. inspect the premises before taking any further action
    B. immediately request that the appropriate group at the realty board repair the wiring
    C. call the president, at once, to assure him or her that the wiring will be fixed immediately
    D. immediately file a code violation against the premises

12. The bureau of gas and electricity receives a complaint of a street light shining in some- 12.____
one's window.
As the inspector assigned to the complaint, you should

    A. immediately order a shield placed on the offending light
    B. tell the complainant that the problem will be completely resolved
    C. tell the complainant that the light is necessary for safety and that nothing can be done
    D. carefully check the location mentioned in the complaint, especially at night, before making any report or recommendations

13. An electrical contractor explains to you that field conditions prevent him from making an 13.____
installation in accordance with the code.
Your FIRST action should be to

    A. insist that the work be done in accordance with the code immediately
    B. tell the contractor that you will take it upon yourself to approve the change if the work can be done safely by the contractor's men
    C. file a violation against the work
    D. tell the contractor to apply to the code revision and interpretation committee, while you make a complete report and recommendation to your superior

14. You are called by an irate individual complaining that he has received an electrical bill 14.____
that is excessive compared to his bill for the same period one year ago. A PROPER tactful procedure is to

    A. tell the individual that your department has no jurisdiction and hang up
    B. carefully listen to the individual and suggest that the complaint be taken to the utility and indicate that the last resort is the Public Service Commission
    C. tell the individual to have his wiring checked by an electrician
    D. agree with the individual, and suggest that only part of the bill be paid and that a letter pointing out the error be sent to the electric company

15. An irate person complains to you about the waste of public money because the lights on 15.____
a portion of a highway are on during the day.
Your response should be to

    A. agree with the person, but tell him that this matter is not in the bureau's jurisdiction and that nothing can be done to remedy the condition
    B. explain that payment to the electrical utility for the lighting is made on a scheduled basis, and that the matter will be corrected as soon as possible
    C. refer him to someone else
    D. refer him to the electrical utility

16. For safe work in buildings, the code states that portable hand-held drills and saws con- 16.____
nected by cord and plug

    A. need have only two wires in the cord
    B. must always have a ground connection to exposed non-current carrying metal parts
    C. can be used to drill into live bus-bars
    D. need not be grounded if protected by an approved system of double insulation and distinctly so marked

17. A newly installed motor and control with the disconnect not in the line of sight are to be inspected.
    Before starting the inspection, it is ESSENTIAL to

    A. set the motor feeder circuit breaker to off
    B. press the control off button
    C. lock the motor disconnect in the off position
    D. remove the equipment drive belt

18. In order to find a blown cartridge fuse on a three-phase 208/120 volt A.C. panelboard, it is BEST to use

    A. fingers across each fuse
    B. a small neon test lamp connected from the line side of each fuse to ground
    C. a 50-watt 120-volt test lamp placed from ground to the load side of each fuse in turn
    D. an ohmmeter across each fuse on the panelboard

19. In order to pull wires into a conduit which terminates in a live panelboard supplied by 208/120V A.C., it is BEST to use a

    A. non-metallic fishline
    B. length of galvanized steel wire
    C. steel fish tape
    D. length of steel chain

20. A branch circuit which is protected by a plug fuse is to be modified.
    In order to do the job safely, it is BEST to

    A. turn the circuit switch to off before starting work
    B. loosen the fuse before starting work
    C. remove the fuse entirely before starting work
    D. work with the circuit alive

21. The current in a feeder is to be measured by using a clamp-on current transformer and a separate ammeter.
    Before placing the current transformer over the feeder,

    A. no special precautions need be taken
    B. the transformer secondary must be short-circuited
    C. the feeder must be disconnected
    D. the transformer secondary must be open-circuited

22. A workman is found to be in contact with live electrical equipment.
    The FIRST thing that a rescuer must do is to

    A. apply artificial respiration
    B. grab the victim around the waist and remove him from the equipment
    C. call an ambulance
    D. disconnect the equipment by any means or remove the victim using rubber gloves

23. Of the following types of wiring methods, the one which must be used in a Class I hazardous location is

    A. electrical metallic tubing with pressure fittings
    B. armored cable
    C. non-metallic sheathed cable
    D. rigid conduit with explosion-proof joints and fittings

24. An electrician falls off a scaffold. He is semi-conscious and breathing. The FIRST thing that should be done is to

    A. move the victim to a sheltered place
    B. force whiskey or brandy into his mouth
    C. start artificial respiration
    D. keep the injured person lying down in a comfortable position with his lead level with his body

25. Of the following statements concerning the installation of lamp holding devices in basements, the one that is CORRECT is that they

    A. shall be porcelain or bakelite
    B. shall not be key-operated
    C. may have metal shells
    D. shall not be pullchain-operated

KEY (CORRECT ANSWERS)

1.	A	11.	A
2.	B	12.	D
3.	C	13.	D
4.	B	14.	B
5.	A	15.	B
6.	C	16.	D
7.	D	17.	C
8.	B	18.	C
9.	A	19.	A
10.	D	20.	C

21.	B
22.	D
23.	D
24.	D
25.	A

EXAMINATION SECTION
TEST 1

DIRECTIONS: Each question or incomplete statement is followed by several suggested answers or completions. Select the one that BEST answers the question or completes the statement. *PRINT THE LETTER OF THE CORRECT ANSWER IN THE SPACE AT THE RIGHT.*

1. The electrical instrument which is used to determine the value of a resistance in excess of one megohm is a

    A. rectifier bridge
    B. high resistance voltmeter
    C. Kelvin balance
    D. Maxwell bridge

    1.____

2. A given D.C. shunt motor, when in operation, rotates clock-wise. If the twoline leads to this motor are interchanged and it is placed back on the line, it will

    A. not operate
    B. rotate counter clock-wise
    C. operate at reduced speed
    D. rotate clock-wise

    2.____

3. In order to start and stop a motor independently from three locations, you would use

    A. three S.P.S.T. switches
    B. one S.P.S.T. switch and two 3-way switches
    C. two 4-way switches and one S.P.S.T. switch
    D. three start-stop push buttons

    3.____

4. When making accurate resistance measurements of metallic electrical conductors, which one of the following is *most important* and should be specified?

    A. Temperature of conductor
    B. Barometric pressure in the test room
    C. Relative humidity in the test room
    D. P.H. of the electrolyte of the battery used in the test

    4.____

5. According to the electrical code, the minimum size of feeders is calculated on the basis of

    A. occupancy and number of cubic feet
    B. occupancy and number of floors
    C. occupancy and number of square feet
    D. occupancy alone

    5.____

6. The diameter of No. 10 AWG is 101.9 mils. The wire whose diameter is 204.3 mils is

    A. No. 8 AWG   B. No. 6 AWG   C. No. 4 AWG   D. No. 2 AWG

    6.____

7. Which one of the following statements is NOT correct?

    A. The ohm is a unit of conductance
    B. The electrolyte in a lead-acid battery is always nitric acid whose specific gravity is 2.0
    C. For batteries with potential limited to 250 volts, cells in sealed glass jars shall require no additional insulation
    D. In garages, cutouts and switches attached to portable apparatus shall be placed in cabinets

    7.____

2 (#1)

8. Which one of the following is CORRECT? 8.___

   A. The resistance of two resistors in parallel is greater than the resistance of either of these resistors
   B. Transformers operating in parallel must have the same ratio of transformation
   C. The farad is a unit of inductance
   D. Transformers change A.C. to D.C.

9. A quantity of light, when uniformly distributed over a one-square foot surface, produces an illumination of one foot-candle on every point of the surface. This quantity of light is called 9.___

   A. candle power   B. a lumen
   C. a gauss   D. the density

10. The word "malleable" means, most nearly, 10.___

    A. capable of being fractured easily
    B. capable of being shaped by beating with a hammer
    C. capable of being case hardened by beating with a hammer
    D. capable of being made flexible by cooling

11. The word "ductile" means, most nearly, 11.___

    A. capable of being fractured easily
    B. capable of being made very hard by heating
    C. capable of springing back to its original shape after a deforming force is removed
    D. capable of being drawn out or hammered thin

12. The process of reducing the brittleness of steel is called 12.___

    A. oxidizing   B. annealing   C. case hardening   D. anodizing

13. An ideal capacitor "A" whose reactance is 2 ohms is connected in parallel with a capacitor whose impedance is 3 ohms. The reactance in ohms of the two capacitors in parallel is, most nearly, 13.___

    A. 1/5   B. 1   C. 6/5   D. 5

14. Which one of the following meters measures energy directly? 14.___

    A. Wattmeter   B. Galvanometer   C. Watt-hour meter   D. Var-meter

15. Which one of the following meters measures power directly? 15.___

    A. Q-meter   B. Wattmeter
    C. Watt-hour meter   D. Ballistic galvanometer

16. A bank of three transformers connected in delta-delta operating on a 240-volt, 3-phase, 60-cycle supply circuit, feeds a certain load. If the supply is changed to 416 volts, 3-phase, 60-cycles, but the load remains unchanged, this transformer bank may be used by connecting it 16.___

    A. Y-Y   B. Δ-Y   C. Y-Δ   D. Δ-Δ

17. A cable having 19 strands each 145 mils in diameter has a circular mil area of, approximately,

    A. 2,800 B. 21,000 C. 300,000 D. 400,000

18. The power loss, in watts, in a conductor is found by

    A. dividing the square of the voltage drop by its resistance
    B. multiplying its resistance by the current
    C. dividing the voltage drop by the current
    D. squaring its resistance and dividing by the current

19. A 220-volt, 3-phase, 10 HP A.C. motor has an efficiency of 80% and a power factor of 70%. The power input at full load for this motor is approximately.

    A. 7 KW B. 9 KW C. 11 KW D. 13 KW

20. The line current drawn at full load by the motor specified in question 19 is most nearly

    A. 28 B. 35 C. 44 D. 57

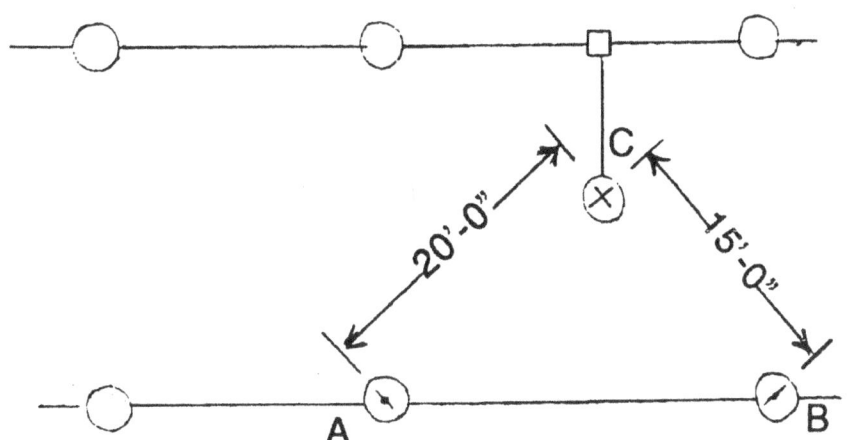

21. In the above ceiling plan, the shortest distance between outlet C and conduit AB is 12 ft. The length AB is approximately,

    A. 35 ft. B. 30 ft. C. 25 ft. D. 22 ft.

22. Which one of the following statements in NOT correct?

    A. Disconnecting switches in series with circuit breakers are usually provided in high voltage circuits for added safety
    B. Underfloor raceways shall be laid so that a straight line from the center of one junction box to the center of the next junction box Shall coincide with the center line of the raceway system
    C. The electrical code allows the presence of exposed live parts in hazardous locations only if they are properly grounded.
    D. According to the electrical code, open wires located in damp places shall be so placed that an air space will be permanently maintained between them and pipes which they cross.

QUESTIONS 23-25.

Questions 23-25 shall be answered in accordance with the paragraph immediately below:

Thermal cutouts, thermal relays, and other devices used for motor running protection... shall be installed in suitable enclosures. They shall be protected by fuses or circuit breakers having ratings or settings not in excess of four times the motor full load current except as permitted in section B30-84.0b2 of this article, exception one, for group installations.

23. The word "thermal," as used above, means, most nearly,   23.____

   A. relating to current
   B. relating to heat or temperature
   C. relating to time
   D. relating to speed

24. The term "circuit breakers," as used above, means, most nearly, devices designed to trip out   24.____

   A. after a certain time
   B. at a predetermined temperature
   C. on a predetermined current overload
   D. at a predetermined speed

25. The above paragraph implies that   25.____

   A. thermal cutouts and thermal relays give motors complete protection from all abnormal conditions
   B. thermal cutouts and thermal relays alone protect motors from short circuits
   C. thermal cutouts and thermal relays alone do not give complete protection but must be supplemented by some form of protection against predetermined overloads
   D. fuses and circuit breakers will protect motors from small but sustained overloads only

26. A 10 KVA transformer has a primary to secondary turn ratio of 10 : 1, 200 turns in the secondary and 1.10 volts per turn. Assuming ideal conditions, the current (in amperes) in the primary winding is, most nearly,   26.____

   A. 4.55   B. 45.5   C. 455.0   D. 0.455

27. Which one of the following statements is FALSE?   27.____

   A. A single pole switch may be installed in the grounded conductor of a circuit
   B. The resistance of a conductor increases as its length increases
   C. Single throw-knife switches shall be so placed that gravity does not tend to close them
   D. Three way and four-way switches shall be classed as singlepole switches

28. The insulation resistance of a certain rubber-insulated single conductor cable 2000-ft. long is found to be 350 megohms. If a 1000ft. section of this cable were cut off, the insulation resistance of this section would be, most nearly,   28.____

   A. 175 megohms   B. 350 megohms
   C. 700 megohms   D. 1400 megohms

29. A one-to-one ratio transformer would, *most likely*, be used to

   A. connect voltmeters to high potential
   B. connect voltmeters to low potential
   C. change from two-phase to three-phase
   D. electrically isolate the load from the source of supply

30. The power factor in a 3 φ A.C. circuit is

   A. apparent watts times true watts
   B. watts divided by the $\sqrt{3}\ E_L\ I_L$
   C. watts divided by $E_L\ I_L$
   D. KVA divided by watts

31. It is proposed to use a 25-cycle 10 KVA, 220/110 volt transformer on a 60-cycle supply instead of purchasing a 60-cycle 10 KVA, 220/110 volt transformer. You, as a supervisor, are consulted on this matter. You should

   A. disapprove unconditionally
   B. approve or disapprove, depending on whether the new load is over or under 1/2 of the former load
   C. approve unconditionally
   D. disapprove because the primary voltage should be lowered

32. The rating, in amperes, of contractors for motors can be determined from their
   A. RMA contactor size
   B. NEMA contactor size
   C. ARMA contactor size
   D. ASEE contactor size

33. The maximum safe current that may flow in any part of the winding of the auto transformer shown above is 50 amperes. As a supervisor, you are consulted as to the safety of this hookup. You should rule that the transformer is

   A. *safe* because the current in winding AB is only 20 amperes
   B. *overloaded* because the current in winding BC is 120 amperes
   C. *unsafe* because the current in winding BC is 100 amperes
   D. *overloaded* because the current in winding BC is 80 amperes

34. Crew "A" alone can do an inspection job in 4 days. Crew "B" alone can do the same job in 2 days. How many days will it take crews "A" and "B" working together to do this job, assuming that they can work together without interference?

   A. 4   B. 3/2   C. 5/3   D. 4/3

35. A resistance of 2 ohms and a resistance of 3 ohms are connected in parallel. The resistance, in ohms, which should be connected in parallel with the above combination in order that the resulting resistance shall be 1 ohm is, most nearly,

    A. 5   B. 6   C. 8   D. 9

35. ___

KEY (CORRECT ANSWERS)

1.	B	16.	C
2.	D	17.	D
3.	D	18.	A
4.	A	19.	B
5.	C	20.	B
6.	C	21.	C
7.	B	22.	C
8.	B	23.	B
9.	B	24.	C
10.	B	25.	C
11.	D	26.	A
12.	B	27.	A
13.	C	28.	C
14.	C	29.	D
15.	B	30.	B

31. A
32. B
33. D
34. D
35. B

EXAMINATION SECTION
TEST 1

DIRECTIONS: Each question or incomplete statement is followed by several suggested answers or completions. Select the one that *BEST* answers the question or completes the statement. *PRINT THE LETTER OF THE CORRECT ANSWER IN THE SPACE AT THE RIGHT.*

1. That system of electric braking in which the traction motors are used as generators and the kinetic energy of the load is used as the actuating means for exerting a retarding force is known as _____ braking.

    A. track   B. magnetic   C. dynamic   D. generator

2. Thermal overload protective devices used for motor running protection protect the motor against

    A. a short-circuit
    B. overcurrent at starting
    C. transient overloads
    D. normal operating overloads

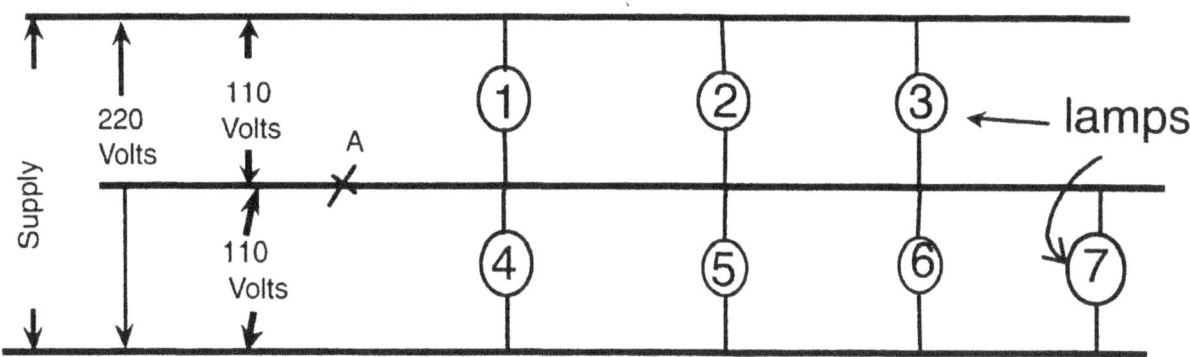

3. In the above diagram, the center conductor breaks at point A.

    A. Lamps 1, 2, and 3 will burn with greater brilliancy than lamps 4, 5, 6 and 7.
    B. Lamps 1, 2, and 3 will burn dimmer than lamps 4, 5, 6, and 7.
    C. All lamps will be extinguished.
    D. All lamps will burn with the same brilliancy that they had before the center lead opened.

4. In ordering standard cartridge fuses it is necessary to specify ONLY the

    A. current capacity
    B. voltage of the circuit
    C. current capacity and the voltage of the circuit
    D. power to be dissipated

5. The current input per phase under rated-load conditions for a 200-H.P., 3 phase, 2300-volt, 0.8 P. F., induction motor which is 90% efficient is _____ amperes.

    A. 52   B. 90   C. 41.6   D. 46.8

6. Referring to problem 5 above, the power input under rated-load conditions is APPROXIMATELY

    A. 149 K.W.   B. 96 K.W.   C. 166 K.W.   D. 332 K.W.

7. Three single-phase transformers are connected in delta on both the primary and secondary sides.
   If one of the transformers burns out the system can continue to operate but its capacity, in terms of the capacity of the original arrangement, is reduced to

   A. 66 2/3%   B. 57.8%   C. 115%   D. 100%

8. In order to successfully operate two compound-wound d.c. generators in parallel it is necessary to use

   A. a compensating winding
   B. an equalizer connection
   C. a series field diverter
   D. commutating poles

9. If a given machine requires a full-load torque of 30 pound-feet and runs at a speed of 1800 R.P.M., the size of direct-coupled motor required to drive this machine is APPROXIMATELY _____ H.P.

   A. 10.3   B. 20.6   C. 15.3   D. 5.2

10. Oil is used in many large transformers to

    A. lubricate the core
    B. lubricate the coils
    C. insulate the coils
    D. insulate the core

11. A certain machine is driven by a 1750-R.P.M. d.c. shunt motor. If the power supply is to be changed to three-phase, 60 cycles, a.c., the MOST suitable replacement motor would be a _____ motor.

    A. series
    B. repulsion
    C. squirrel-cage induction
    D. capacitor

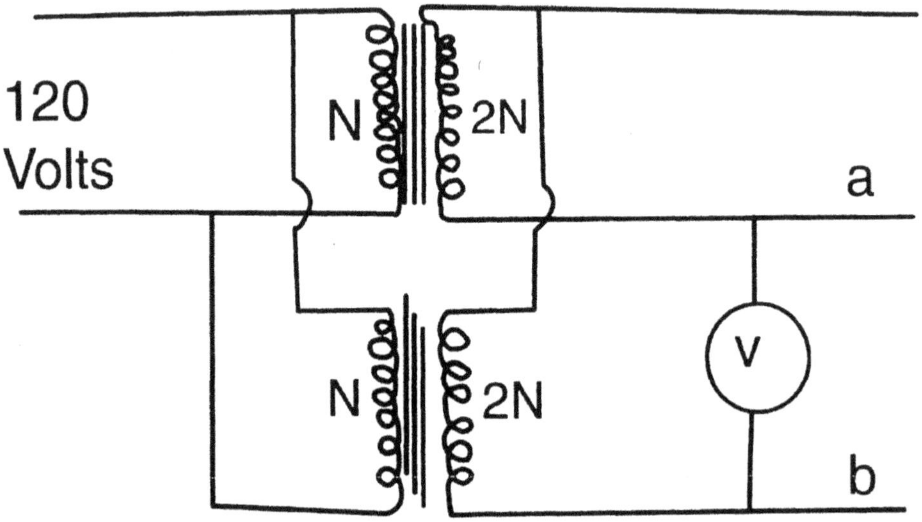

12. Two transformers with ratios of 1.2 are to be connected in parallel. To test for proper connections the circuit of the above diagram is used.
    The transformers may be connected in parallel by connecting lead a to lead b if the voltmeter shown reads _____ volts.

    A. 120   B. 240   C. zero   D. 480

13. You were asked to calculate the electric bill for the last month. The kilowatt-hour meter reads 99,010 K.W.-hrs. at the end of the previous month and now reads 00,110 K.W.-hrs. The demand meter reads 75 K.W.
    The energy rate is:
    For the first 500 K.W.-hrs. $0.04 per K.W.-hr.
    For the next 300 K.W.-hrs. $0.03 per K.W.-hr.
    For the next 200 K.W.-hrs. $0.02 per K.W.-hr.
    For all in excess of 100 K.W.-hrs. $0.01 per K.W.-hr.
    The demand rate is $0.50 per K.W.
    The total electric bill is

    A. $71.50   B. $67.50   C. $83.50   D. $74.50

13.____

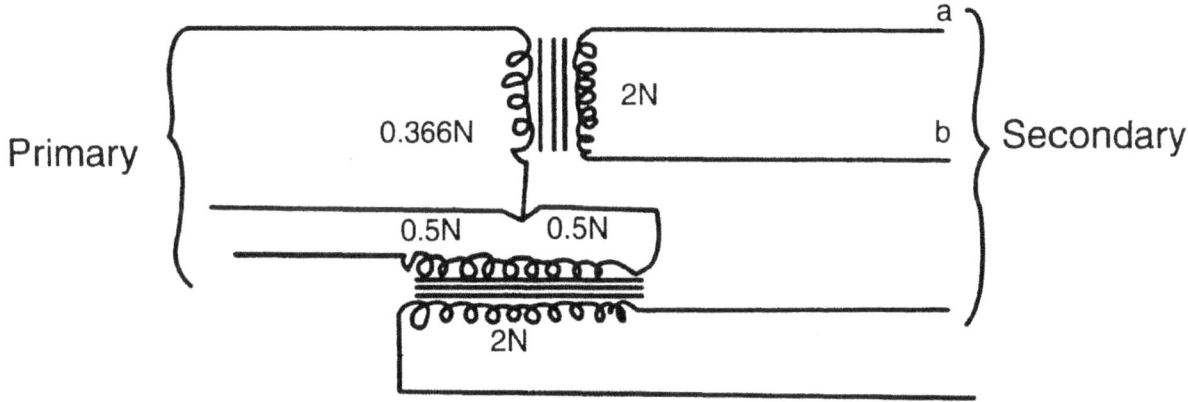

14. If the primary leads in the above diagram are connected to a three-phase, three-wire, 208 volt system and the transformation ratios are as indicated on the diagram, the secondary leads will form a _____ -phase, _____ -wire system.

    A. three   four
    B. two   four
    C. four   five
    D. three   three

14.____

15. In the circuit of the above diagram, the voltage between the secondary leads a and b is _____ volts.

    A. 208   B. 120   C. 416   D. 240

15.____

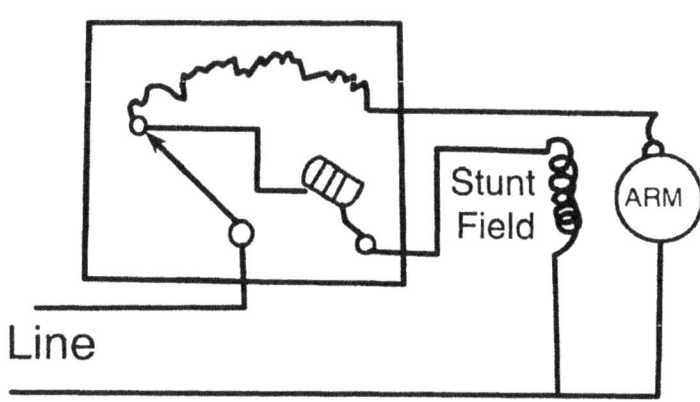

16. The circuit of the above diagram shows a d.c. motor starter.
    One of the features of this starting box is a(n) _____ release.

    A. overload   B. no-field   C. reverse-current   D. underload

17. For starting a three-phase induction motor a three-phase transformer is used with its primaries connected in delta and its secondaries connected in delta for starting and in wye for running.
    The ratio of the running to the starting voltage is

    A. 3 : 1   B. 2 : 1   C. 1.73 : 1   D. 1.41 : 1

18. A booster transformer is a transformer connected

    A. in such a manner as to increase the load on the line by a fixed percentage
    B. as a delta-connected bank
    C. as an auto-transformer to raise the line voltage by a fixed percentage
    D. in such a manner as to raise the frequency by a fixed percentage

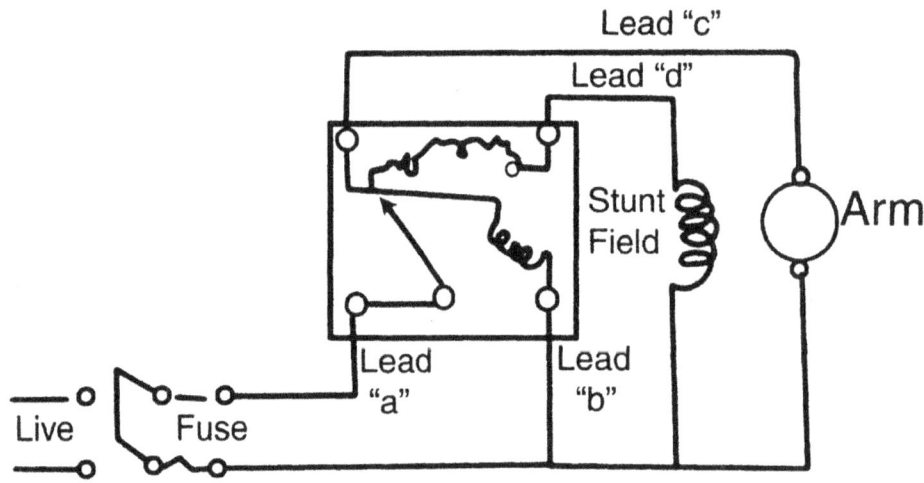

19. The motor shown in the above figure does not operate correctly. When the line switch is closed the fuses blow.
    To correct this fault leads _____ and _____ should be interchanged.

    A. leads *a* and *b*
    B. leads *a* and *c*
    C. leads *b* and *d*
    D. leads *c* and *d*

20. A standard stranded cable contains 19 strands. When measured with a micrometer the diameter of each strand is found to be 105.5 mils.
    If, under certain conditions, the allowable current density is 600 C.M. per ampere the allowable current-carrying capacity of this conductor is _____ amperes.

    A. 236   B. 176.3   C. 352.5   D. 705

21. For MAXIMUM safety the magnetic contactors used for reversing the direction of rotation of a motor should be

    A. electrically interlocked
    B. electrically and mechanically interlocked
    C. mechanically interlocked
    D. operated from independent sources

22. When the starter for a 250-volt, direct-current shunt motor whose full-load armature current is 20 amperes, is in the first contact postion, the total resistance in the armature circuit, to permit the motor to start with 150% of rated torque, should be APPROXIMATELY _____ ohms.

    A. 5   B. 8   C. 12   D. 20

23. If the allowable current density for copper bus bars is 1000 amperes per square inch, the current-carrying capacity of a circular copper bar having a diameter of two inches is APPROXIMATELY _____ amperes.

    A. 1050   B. 2320   C. 3140   D. 4260

24. A rotary converter, operating at unity power factor, may be made to take a leading power factor by

    A. *increasing* the d.c. field strength of the machine
    B. *decreasing* the d.c. field strength of the machine
    C. *decreasing* the speed at which it operates
    D. *increasing* the speed at which it operates

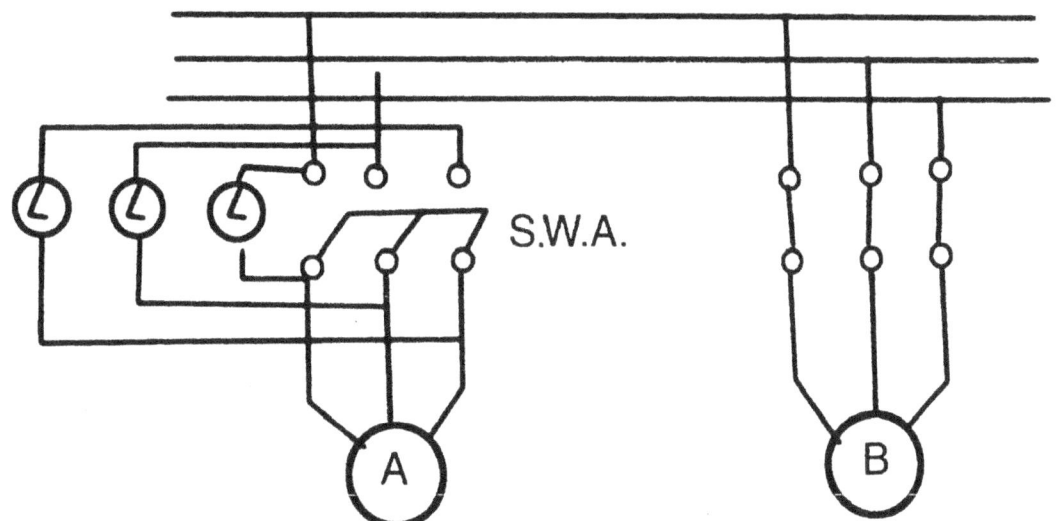

25. Two alternators are to be synchronized for parallel operation, the correct synchronization being indicated by three lamps, as shown in the above diagram.
    The CORRECT time to close switch A is

    A. when the lamps are at maximum brilliancy
    B. when the lamps are dark
    C. just before the lamps reach maximum brilliancy
    D. just after the lamps reach maximum brilliancy

26. The maximum voltage-drop between a d.c. motor and switchboard is not to exceed one percent of the supply voltage.
If the supply voltage is 200 volts, the full-load current of the motor 100 amperes, the distance from the switchboard to the motor 100 feet, and the resistivity of copper 10 ohms per C.M.-foot, the size wire required in C.M. is

   A. 25,000   B. 50,000   C. 100,000   D. 200,000

27. One foot of a certain size of nichrome wire has a resistance of 1.63 ohms.
To make a heating element for a toaster that will use 5 amperes at 110 volts, the number of feet of wire needed is APPROXIMATELY

   A. 17.9   B. 8.2   C. 5.5   D. 13.5

28. A tri-free circuit breaker is one that

   A. is tripped from a shunt-circuit through a relay
   B. can be tripped only by an operator
   C. cannot be tripped when the operating lever is held in the closed position
   D. can be tripped by the overload mechanism even though the operating lever is held in the closed position

29. The following equipment is required for a *2-line return-call* electric bell circuit: 2 bells, 2 metallic lines,

   A. 2 ordinary push-buttons, and one set of batteries
   B. 2 return-call push-buttons and 2 sets of batteries
   C. 2 return-call push-buttons and one set of batteries
   D. one ordinary push-button, one return-call push button and one set of batteries

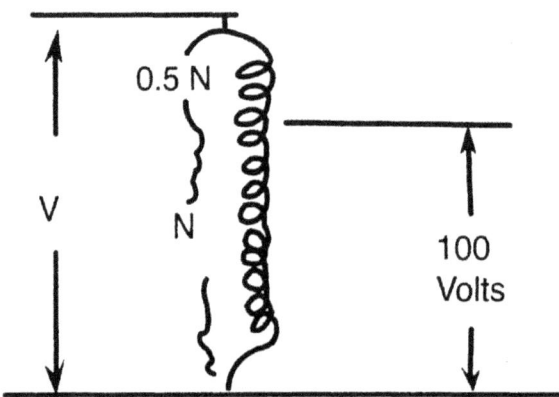

30. An auto-transformer with turns ratio as indicated in the above sketch is connected to a 100-volt, 60-cycle supply on the low-tension side.
The voltage, V, on the high tension side is _____ volts.

   A. 50   B. 100   C. 150   D. 200

31. The MINIMUM size of grounding conductor for a direct or alternating-current system is

   A. No. 14   B. No. 10   C. No. 8   D. No. 6

32. The thickness of insulation for a No. 8 rubber-covered conductor for use at NOT more than 2000 volts shall be _____ of an inch.

    A. 2/64ths   B. 3/64ths   C. 4/64ths   D. 5/64ths

33. A gutter whose width is 36 inches shall be constructed of sheet metal of thickness NOT less than No. _____ U.S. standard sheet metal gauge.

    A. 10   B. 12   C. 14   D. 16

34. The MAXIMUM voltage permitted on the push buttons of elevator signalling circuits shall be _____ volts to ground.

    A. 300   B. 125   C. 250   D. 600

35. Electric motors installed in hospital operating rooms shall be of the _____ proof type.

    A. water   B. explosion   C. dust   D. light

36. Connecting batteries in parallel instead of in series _____ of the batteries.

    A. *increases* the current output
    B. *decreases* the life
    C. *increases* the voltage
    D. *decreases* the current output

37. To charge a storage battery, one would use

    A. either a.c. or d.c.   B. a.c. only
    C. d.c. only   D. only low frequency a.c.

38. A transformer is USUALLY used to

    A. change a.c. to d.c.
    B. raise or lower a.c. voltage
    C. change d.c. to a.c.
    D. change the frequency of the a.c. supply

39. The commutator of a d.c. generator

    A. keeps the current flowing in one direction in the load circuit
    B. reverses the current direction in the armature
    C. acts only as a sliding electrical contact
    D. changes a.c. to d.c. within the armature

40. The number of fresh dry cells that should be connected in series to obtain 12 volts is

    A. 2   B. 6   C. 8   D. 12

KEY (CORRECT ANSWERS)

1. C	11. C	21. B	31. C
2. D	12. C	22. B	32. D
3. A	13. A	23. C	33. A
4. C	14. B	24. A	34. A
5. A	15. C	25. B	35. B
6. C	16. B	26. C	36. A
7. B	17. C	27. D	37. C
8. B	18. C	28. D	38. B
9. A	19. D	29. B	39. A
10. C	20. C	30. C	40. C

TEST 2

DIRECTIONS: Each question or incomplete statement is followed by several suggested answers or completions. Select the one that *BEST* answers the question or completes the statement. *PRINT THE LETTER OF THE CORRECT ANSWER IN THE SPACE AT THE RIGHT.*

1. Of the following, the BEST conductor of electricity is 1.____

   A. tungsten   B. iron   C. aluminum   D. carbon

2. A 600-volt cartridge fuse is MOST readily distinguished from a 250-volt cartridge fuse of the same ampere rating by comparing the 2.____

   A. insulating materials used   B. shape of the ends
   C. diameters   D. lengths

3. Many power-transformer cases are filled with oil. The purpose of the oil is to 3.____

   A. prevent rusting of the core
   B. reduce a.c. hum
   C. insulate the coils from the case
   D. transmit heat from the coils and core

4. In order to make certain that a 600-volt circuit is dead before working on it, the BEST procedure is to 4.____

   A. test with a voltmeter
   B. *short* the circuit quickly with a piece of insulated wire
   C. see if any of the insulated conductors are warm
   D. disconnect one of the wires of the circuit near the feed

5. When closing an exposed knife switch on a panel, the action should be positive and rapid because there is less likelihood of 5.____

   A. the operator receiving a shock
   B. the operator being burned
   C. the fuse blowing
   D. injury to equipment connected to the circuit

6. Lubrication is never used on 6.____

   A. a knife switch
   B. a die when threading conduit
   C. wires being pulled into a conduit
   D. a commutator

7. If one plug fuse in a 110-volt circuit blows because of a short-circuit, a 110-volt lamp screwed into the fuse socket will 7.____

   A. burn dimly   B. remain dark   C. burn out   D. burn normally

8. Of the following, the LEAST undesirable practice if a specified wire size is not available for part of a circuit is to 8.____

A. use two wires of 1/2 capacity in parallel as a substitute
B. use the next larger size wire
C. use a smaller size wire if the length is short
D. reduce the size of the fuse and use smaller wire

9. If it is necessary to increase slightly the tension of an ordinary coiled spring in a relay, the PROPER procedure is to

   A. cut off one or two turns
   B. compress it slightly
   C. stretch it slightly
   D. unhook one end, twist and replace

9._____

10. As compared with solid wire, stranded wire of the same gage size is

    A. given a higher current rating
    B. easier to skin
    C. larger in total diameter
    D. better for high voltage

10._____

11. Motor frames are USUALLY positively grounded by a special connection in order to

    A. remove static
    B. protect against lightening
    C. provide a neutral
    D. protect against shock

11._____

12. If a live conductor is contacted accidentally, the severity of the electrical shock is determined PRIMARILY by

    A. the size of the conductor
    B. whether the current is a.c. or d.c.
    C. the contact resistance
    D. the current in the conductor

12._____

13. If a snap switch rated at 5 amperes is used for an electric heater which draws 10 amperes, the MOST likely result is that the

    A. circuit fuse will be blown
    B. circuit wiring will become hot
    C. heater output will be halved
    D. switch contacts will become hot

13._____

14. To straighten a long length of wire which has been tightly coiled, before pulling it into a conduit run, a good method is to

    A. roll the wire into a coil in the opposite direction
    B. fasten one end to the floor and whip it against the floor from the other end
    C. draw it over a convenient edge
    D. hold the wire at one end and twist it with the pliers from the other end

14._____

15. The wire size MOST commonly used for branch circuits in residences is

    A. #14   B. #16   C. #12   D. #18

15._____

16. If the applied voltage on an incandescent lamp is increased 10%, the lamp will

    A. have a longer life
    B. burn more brightly
    C. consume less power
    D. fail by insulation breakdown

16._____

17. You would expect that the overload trip coil on an ordinary air circuit breaker would have

    A. heavy wire
    B. fine wire
    C. many turns
    D. heavily insulated wire

18. A cycle counter is an electrical timer which, when energized by alternating current, counts the number of cycles until it is de-energized.
    If a cycle counter is energized from a 60-cycle power supply for ten seconds, the reading of the instrument should be

    A. 6   B. 10   C. 60   D. 600

19. The MOST practical way to determine in the field if a large coil of #14 wire has the required length for a given job is to

    A. weigh the coil
    B. measure one turn and count the turns
    C. unroll it into another coil
    D. make a visual comparison with a full coil

20. A frequency meter is constructed as a potential device, that is, to be connected across the line.
    A logical reason for this is that

    A. only the line voltage has frequency
    B. a transformer may then be used with it
    C. the reading will be independent of the varying current
    D. it is safer than a series device

21. It is usually not safe to connect 110 volts d.c. to a magnet coil designed for 110 volts a.c. because the

    A. insulation is insufficient
    B. iron may overheat
    C. wire may overheat
    D. inductance may be too high

22. The MOST satisfactory temporary replacement for a 40-watt, 120-volt incandescent lamp, if an identical replacement is not available, is a lamp rated at _____ watts, _____ volts.

    A. 100; 240   B. 60; 130   C. 40; 32   D. 15; 120

23. If the following bare copper wire sizes were arranged in the order of increasing weight per 1000 feet, the CORRECT arrangement would be

    A. #00, #40, #8
    B. #40, #00, #8
    C. #00, #8, #40
    D. #40, #8, #00

24. The purpose of having a rheostat in the field circuit of a d.c. shunt motor is to

    A. control the speed of the motor
    B. minimize the starting current
    C. limit the field current to a safe value
    D. reduce sparking at the brushes

25. The resistance of a 1000-ft. length of a certain size copper wire is required to be 10.0 ohms ± 2%.
    This wire would NOT be acceptable if the resistance was _____ ohms.

    A. 10.12   B. 10.02   C. 10.22   D. 9.82

26. The LEAST important action in making a good soldered connection between two wires is to

    A. use the proper flux   B. clean the wires well
    C. use plenty of solder   D. use sufficient heat

27. Of the following, the BEST conductor of electricity is

    A. aluminum   B. carbon   C. copper   D. water

28. Good practice requires that the end of a piece of conduit be reamed after it has been cut to length.
    The purpose of the reaming is to

    A. prevent insulation damage when pulling in the wires
    B. finish the conduit accurately to length
    C. make the threading easier
    D. remove loose rust

29. According to the national electrical code, a run of conduit between two outlet boxes should not contain more than four quarter bends.
    The MOST likely reason for this limitation is that more bends will

    A. result in cracking the conduit
    B. make the pulling of the wire too difficult
    C. increase the wire length unnecessarily
    D. not be possible in one standard length of conduit

30. Asbestos is commonly used as the covering of electric wires in locations where there is likely to be high

    A. voltage   B. temperature   C. humidity   D. current

31. Portable lamp cord is LIKELY to have

    A. steel armor   B. stranded wires
    C. paper insulation   D. number 8 wire

32. The one of the following terms which could NOT correctly be used in describing a knife switch is

    A. quick-break   B. single throw   C. four-pole   D. toggle

33. With respect to common electric light bulbs, it is CORRECT to state that the

    A. circuit voltage has no effect on the life of the bulb
    B. filament is made of carbon
    C. base has a left hand thread
    D. lower wattage bulb has the higher resistance

34. The resistance of a 1000-foot coil of a certain size copper wire is 10 ohms. If 300 feet are cut off, the resistance of the remainder of the coil is _____ ohms.

    A. 7   B. 3   C. 0.7   D. 0.3

35. The term *15 ampere* is COMMONLY used in identifying a(n)

    A. insulator   B. fuse   C. conduit   D. outlet box

36. When connecting the two lead wires of a test instrument to a live d.c. circuit, the BEST procedure is to first make the negative or ground connection and then the positive connection.
    The reason for this procedure is that

    A. electricity flows from positive to negative
    B. there is less danger of accidental shock
    C. the reverse procedure may blow the fuse
    D. less arcing will occur when the connection is made

37. To make a good soldered connection between two stranded wires, it is LEAST important to

    A. twist the wires together before soldering
    B. use enough heat to make the solder flow freely
    C. clean the wires carefully
    D. apply solder to each strand before twisting the two wires together

38. When a step-up transformer is used, it increases the

    A. voltage   B. current   C. power   D. frequency

39. Lock nuts are frequently used in making electrical connections on terminal boards.
    The purpose of such lock nuts is to

    A. make tighter connections with less effort
    B. make it difficult to tamper with the connections
    C. avoid stripping the threads
    D. keep the connections from loosening through vibration

40. The core of an electro-magnet is USUALLY

    A. aluminum   B. lead   C. brass   D. iron

41. A stranded wire is given the same size designation as a solid wire if it has the same

    A. cross-sectional area
    B. weight per foot
    C. overall diameter
    D. strength

42. One advantage of cutting 1" rigid conduit with a hacksaw rather than a 3-wheel pipe cutter is that

    A. the cut can be made with less exertion
    B. the pipe is not squeezed out of round
    C. less reaming is required after the cut
    D. no vise is needed

43. Assume that the field leads of a large, completely disconnected d.c. motor are not tagged or otherwise marked. You could readily tell the shunt field leads from the series field leads by the

    A. length of the leads
    B. size of wire
    C. thickness of insulation
    D. type of insulation

44. Standard electrician's pliers should NOT be used to

    A. bend thin sheet metal
    B. crush insulation on wires to be skinned
    C. cut off nail points sticking through a board
    D. hold a wire in position for soldering

45. The device used to change a.c. to d.c. is a

    A. frequency B. regulator C. transformer D. rectifier

46. The CHIEF advantage of using stranded rather than solid conductors for electrical wiring is that stranded conductors are

    A. more flexible
    B. easier to skin
    C. smaller
    D. stronger

47. One identifying feature of a squirrel-cage induction motor is that it has no

    A. windings on the stationary part
    B. commutator or slip rings
    C. air gap
    D. iron core in the rotating part

48. If a cartridge fuse is hot to the touch when you remove it to do some maintenance on the circuit, this MOST probably indicates that the

    A. voltage of the circuit is too high
    B. fuse clips do not make good contact
    C. equipment on the circuit starts and stops frequently
    D. fuse is oversize for the circuit

49. The instrument MOST commonly used to determine the state of charge of a lead-acid storage battery is the

    A. thermometer
    B. hydrometer
    C. voltmeter
    D. ammeter

50. Rigid conduit must be installed as to prevent the collection of water in it between outlets. In order to meet this requirement, the conduit should NOT have a

    A. low point between successive outlets
    B. high point between successive outlets
    C. low point at an outlet
    D. high point at an outlet

KEY (CORRECT ANSWERS)

1. C	11. D	21. C	31. B	41. A
2. D	12. C	22. B	32. D	42. C
3. D	13. D	23. D	33. D	43. B
4. A	14. B	24. A	34. A	44. C
5. B	15. A	25. C	35. B	45. D
6. D	16. C	26. C	36. B	46. A
7. D	17. A	27. C	37. D	47. B
8. B	18. D	28. A	38. A	48. B
9. A	19. B	29. B	39. D	49. B
10. C	20. C	30. B	40. D	50. A

TEST 3

DIRECTIONS: Each question or incomplete statement is followed by several suggested answers or completions. Select the one that BEST answers the question or completes the statement. PRINT THE LETTER OF THE CORRECT ANSWER IN THE SPACE AT THE RIGHT.

1. When a test lamp is connected to the two ends of a cartridge fuse on an operating switchboard, the indication in ALL cases will be that this fuse is

   A. blown if the test lamp remains dark
   B. good if the test lamp lights
   C. blown if the test lamp lights
   D. good if the test lamp remains dark

   1.____

2. If one copper wire has a diameter of 0.128 inch, and another copper wire has a diameter of 0.064 inch, the resistance of 1,000 feet of the first wire compared to the same length of the second wire is

   A. one half   B. one quarter   C. double   D. four times

   2.____

3. If the allowable current in a copper bus bar is 1,000 amperes per square inch of cross-section, the width of a standard 1/4" bus bar designed to carry 1500 amperes would be

   A. 2"   B. 4"   C. 6"   D. 8"

   3.____

4. It is not possible to obtain a 200-watt light-bulb that is as small in all dimensions as the standard 150-watt light-bulb.
   The PRINCIPAL advantage to users resulting from this reduction in size is that

   A. maintenance electricians can carry many more light-bulbs
   B. two sizes of light-bulbs can be kept in the same storage space
   C. the higher wattage bulb can now fit into certain lighting fixtures
   D. less breakage is apt to occur in handling

   4.____

5. A carbon brush in a d.c. motor should exert a pressure of about 1 1/2 lbs. per square inch on the commutator.
   A much lighter pressure would be MOST likely to result in

   A. sparking at the commutator
   B. vibration of the armature
   C. the brush getting out of line
   D. excessive wear of the brush holder

   5.____

6. The number of watts of heat given off by a resistor is expressed by the formula I^2R.
   If 10 volts is applied to a 5-ohm resistor, the heat given off will be _____ watts.

   A. 500   B. 250   C. 50   D. 20

   6.____

7. When a number of rubber insulated wires are being pulled into a run of conduit having several sharp bends between the two pull boxes, the pulling is likely to be hard and the wires are subjected to considerable strain.
   For these reasons it is ADVISABLE in such a case to

   7.____

A. push the wires into the feed end of the conduit at the same time that pulling is being done
B. pull in only one wire at a time
C. use extra heavy grease
D. pull the wires back a few inches after each forward pull to gain momentum

8. The plug of a portable tool should be removed from the convenience outlet by grasping the plug and not by pulling on the cord because   8.____

   A. the plug is easier to grip than the cord
   B. pulling on the cord may allow the plug to fall on the floor and break
   C. pulling on the cord may break the wires off the plug terminals
   D. the plug is generally better insulated than the cord

9. When using a pipe wrench, the hand should be placed so as to pull instead of push on the wrench.   9.____
   The basis for this recommendation is that there is less likelihood of

   A. the wrench slipping
   B. injury to the hand if the wrench slips
   C. injury to the pipe if the wrench slips
   D. stripped pipe threads

10. High voltage switches in power plants are commonly so constructed that their contacts are submerged in oil.   10.____
    The purpose of the oil is to

    A. help quench arcing
    B. lubricate the contacts
    C. cool the switch mechanism
    D. insulate the contacts from the switch framework

11. In a storage battery installation consisting of twenty 2-volt cells connected in series, a leak develops in one of the cells and all the electrolyte runs out of it.   11.____
    The terminal voltage across the twenty cells will now be

    A. 40   B. 38   C. 2   D. 0

12. When removing the insulation from a wire before making a splice, care should be taken to avoid nicking the wire MAINLY because then the   12.____

    A. current carrying capacity will be reduced
    B. resistance will be increased
    C. insulation will be harder to remove
    D. wire is more likely to break

13. Good practice dictates that an adjustable open-end wrench should be used PRIMARILY when the   13.____

    A. nut to be turned is soft and must not be scored
    B. proper size of fixed wrench is not available
    C. extra leverage is needed
    D. location is cramped permitting only a small turning angle

14. It would generally be poor practice to use ordinary slip-joint pliers to

    A. pull a small nail
    B. bend a wire
    C. remove a cotter pin
    D. tighten a machine bolt

15. The a.c. motor which has exactly the same speed at full-load as at no load is the _____ motor.

    A. synchronous   B. repulsion   C. induction   D. condenser

16. A metal bushing is usually screwed on to the end of rigid conduit inside of a junction box. The bushing serves to

    A. center the wires in the conduit
    B. separate the wires where they leave the conduit
    C. protect the wires against abrasion
    D. prevent sagging of the conduit

17. The PROPER abrasive for cleaning the commutator of a d.c. generator is

    A. steel wool   B. emery cloth   C. sand paper   D. soapstone

18. If a *live* 120-volt d.c. lighting circuit is connected to the 120-volt winding of an otherwise disconnected power transformer, the result will be

    A. blowing of the d.c. circuit fuse
    B. magnetization of the transformer fuse
    C. sparking at the transformer secondary terminals
    D. burning out of lights on the d.c. circuit

19. Threaded joints in rigid conduit runs are made watertight through the use

    A. petroleum jelly   B. solder   C. red lead   D. paraffin wax

20. The letters S.P.S.T. frequently found on wiring plans refer to a type of

    A. cable   B. switch   C. fuse   D. motor

21. Renewable fuses differ from ordinary fuses in that

    A. they can carry higher overloads
    B. burned out fuses can be located more easily
    C. burned out fuse elements can be readily replaced
    D. they can be used on higher voltages

22. After No. 10 A.W.G., the next SMALLER copper wire size in common use is No.

    A. 8   B. 9   C. 11   D. 12

23. The BEST of the following tools to use for cutting off a piece of single-conductor #6 rubber insulated lead covered cable is

    A. pair of electrician's pliers
    B. hacksaw
    C. hammer and cold chisel
    D. lead knife

24. Toggle bolts are MOST appropriate for use to fasten conduit clamps to a

    A. steel column
    B. concrete wall
    C. hollow tile wall
    D. brick wall

25. If a 10-24 by 3/4" machine screw is not available, the screw which could be MOST easily modified to use in an emergency is a

    A. 10-24 by 1/2"
    B. 12-24 by 3/4"
    C. 10-24 by 1 1/2"
    D. 8-24 by 3/4"

26. A standard pipe thread differs from a standard screw thread in that the pipe thread

    A. is tapered
    B. is deeper
    C. requires no lubrication when cutting
    D. has the same pitch for any diameter of pipe

27. The material which is LEAST likely to be found in use as the outer covering of rubber insulated wires or cables is

    A. cotton
    B. varnished cambric
    C. lead
    D. neoprene

28. In measuring to determine the size of a stranded insulated conductor, the proper place to use the wire gauge is on

    A. the insulation
    B. the outer covering
    C. the stranded conductor
    D. one strand of the conductor

29. Rubber insulation on an electrical conductor would MOST quickly be damaged by continuous contact with

    A. acid
    B. water
    C. oil
    D. alkali

30. If a fuse clip becomes hot under normal circuit load, the MOST probable cause is that the

    A. clip makes poor contact with the fuse ferrule
    B. circuit wires are too small
    C. current rating of the fuse is too high
    D. voltage rating of the fuse is too low

31. If the input ot a 10 to 1 step-down transformer is 15 amperes at 2400 volts, the secondary output would be NEAREST to _____ amperes at _____ volts.

    A. 1.5; 24,000
    B. 150; 240
    C. 1.5; 240
    D. 150; 24,000

32. The resistance of a copper wire to the flow of electricity

    A. *increases* as the diameter of the wire increases
    B. *decreases* as the diameter of the wire decreases
    C. *decreases* as the length of the wire increases
    D. *increases* as the length of the wire increases

33. Where galvanized steel conduit is used, the PRIMARY purpose of the galvanizing is to

   A. increase mechanical strength
   B. retard rusting
   C. provide a good surface for painting
   D. provide good electrical contact for grounding

34. The CORRECT method of measuring the power taken by an a.c electric motor is to use a

   A. wattmeter
   B. voltmeter and an ammeter
   C. power factor meter
   D. tachometer

35. Checking a piece of rigid electrical conduit with a steel scale, you measure the inside diameter as 1 1/16" and the outside diameter as 1 5/16".
   The NOMINAL size of this conduit is

   A. 3/4" B. 1" C. 1 1/4" D. 1 1/2"

36. Of the following, it would be MOST difficult to solder a copper wire to a metal plate made of

   A. copper B. brass C. iron D. tin

37. After a piece of rigid conduit has been cut to length, it is MOST important to

   A. ream the inside edge to prevent injury to wires
   B. file the end flat to make an accurate fit
   C. coat the cut surface with red lead to prevent rust
   D. rile the outside edge to a taper for ease in threading

38. Rigid conduit is generally secured to sheet metal outlet boxes by means of

   A. threadless couplings
   B. box connectors
   C. locknuts and bushings
   D. conduit clamps

39. While a certain d.c. shunt motor is driving a light load, part of the field winding becomes short circuited,
   The motor will MOST likely

   A. increase its speed
   B. decrease its speed
   C. remain at the same speed
   D. come to a stop

40. Each time a certain electric heater is turned on, the incandescent lights connected to the same branch circuit become dimmer and when the heater is turned off the lamps become brighter.
   The factor which probably contributes MOST to this effect is the

   A. voltage of the circuit
   B. size of the circuit fuse
   C. current taken by the lamps
   D. size of the circuit conductors

41. Comparing the shunt field winding with the series field winding of a compound d.c. motor, it would be CORRECT to say that the shunt field winding has _____ resistance,

   A. *more* turns but the *lower*
   B. *more* turns and the *higher*
   C. *fewer* turns and the *lower*
   D. *fewer* turns but the *higher*

42. The most important reason for using a fuse-puller when removing a cartridge fuse from the fuse clips is to

    A. prevent blowing of the fuse
    B. prevent injury to the fuse element
    C. reduce the chances of personal injury
    D. reduce arcing at the fuse clips

43. A coil of wire wound on an iron core draws exactly 5 amperes when connected across the terminals of a ten-volt storage battery.
    If this coil is now connected across the ten-volt secondary terminals of an ordinary power transformer, the current drawn will be

    A. *less* than 5 amperes
    B. *more* than 5 amperes
    C. *exactly* 5 amperes
    D. more or less than 5 amperes depending on the frequency

44. A revolution counter applied to the end of a rotating shaft reads 100 when a stop-watch is started. It reads 850 when the stop-watch indicates 90 seconds.
    The average RPM of the shaft is

    A. 8.4   B. 9.4   C. 500   D. 567

45. Motor speeds are generally measured directly in RPM by the use of a

    A. potentiometer   B. manometer   C. dynamometer   D. tachometer

46. To reverse the direction of rotation of a 3-phase motor, it is necessary to

    A. increase the resistance of the rotor circuit
    B. interchange any two of the three line connections
    C. interchange all three line connections
    D. reverse the polarity of the rotor circuit

47. Mica is commonly used in electrical construction for

    A. commutator bar separators   B. switchboard panels
    C. strain insulators   D. heater cord insulation

48. The rating term *1000 ohms, 10 watts* would generally be applied to a

    A. heater   B. relay   C. resistor   D. transformer

49. According to the National Electrical Code, the identified (or grounded) conductor of the branch circuit supplying an incandescent lamp socket must be connected to the screw shell.
    The MOST likely reason for this requirement is that

    A. longer lamp life results
    B. the wiring will be kept more nearly uniform
    C. persons are more likely to come in contact with the shell
    D. the shell can carry heavier currents

50. In an installation used to charge a storage battery from a motor-generator you would LEAST expect to find a(n)

    A. rectifier   B. rheostat   C. voltmeter   D. ammeter

KEY (CORRECT ANSWERS)

1. C	11. D	21. C	31. B	41. B
2. B	12. D	22. D	32. D	42. C
3. C	13. B	23. B	33. B	43. A
4. C	14. D	24. C	34. A	44. C
5. A	15. A	25. C	35. B	45. D
6. D	16. C	26. A	36. C	46. B
7. A	17. C	27. B	37. A	47. A
8. C	18. A	28. D	38. C	48. C
9. B	19. C	29. C	39. A	49. C
10. A	20. B	30. A	40. D	50. A

WORK SCHEDULING
EXAMINATION SECTION
TEST 1

DIRECTIONS: Each question or incomplete statement is followed by several suggested answers or completions. Select the one that BEST answers the question or completes the statement. *PRINT THE LETTER OF THE CORRECT ANSWER IN THE SPACE AT THE RIGHT.*

Questions 1-8.

DIRECTIONS: Questions 1 through 8 are to be answered on the basis of the following information.

Assume that you are the supervisor of a unit that works seven days a week. You need to determine the work and vacation schedules of the employees you supervise for the month of July.

THE EMPLOYEES

Alan W.	9 years seniority	computer operator
Jane B.	4 1/2 years seniority	typist
Alex H.	5 years seniority	security staff
Tony E.	4 years seniority	security staff
Andre T.	4 2/3 years seniority	typist
Mary W.	11 years seniority	security staff
Andy R.	13 years seniority	computer operator
Rhonda L.	2 years seniority	computer operator
Ethel R.	15 years seniority	typist
Roger G.	3 years seniority	security staff

THE VACATION PREFERENCES OF THE EMPLOYEES:

	1st vacation day	1ast vacation day
Alan W.	7/1	7/19
Jane B.	7/15	7/29
Alex H.	7/8	7/22
Tony E.	7/22	7/30
Andre T.	7/1	7/14
Mary W.	7/1	7/22
Andy R.	7/15	7/30
Rhonda L.	7/20	7/31
Ethel R.	7/1	7/27
Roger G.	7/21	7/31

IMPORTANT REGULATIONS REGARDING VACATION LEAVE

Employees with seniority have first choice for their preferred vacation dates. Seniority should be calculated separately for each of the three occupational groups.

2 (#1)

There must be two security employees on duty each working day in July. This overrides any other considerations.

There must be one typist on duty each working day in July. This overrides any other considerations.

Employees with least seniority, when denied their first choice of vacation dates, should automatically be scheduled ahead for vacation on the very next date closest to the dates they had originally preferred and the length of the vacation extended the appropriate number of days. Example: A vacation originally requested for 7/13, but changed because of seniority, would be moved AHEAD to a date after 7/13 (to 7/16, for example).

You may want to use the calendar below to help you organize this information.
JULY

1	2	3	4	5	6	7
8	9	10	11	12	13	14
15	16	17	18	19	20	21
22	23	24	25	26	27	28
29	30	31				

1. The number of employees on vacation on July 16 should be   1.____
    A. four   B. five   C. six   D. seven

2. The number of employees on vacation on July 22 should be   2.____
    A. five   B. six   C. seven   D. eight

3. How many typists will be working on July 15?   3.____
    A. One   B. Two   C. Three   D. None

4. How many workers will be on vacation on July 31?   4.____
    A. Two   B. Three   C. Four   D. Five

5. Which of the following is TRUE of the employees in the unit?   5.____
    I. Andy R., Jane B., Tony E., and Mary W. will be on vacation on 7/22.
    II. Ethel R., Andre T., Mary W., and Alex H. will be on vacation on 7/8.

III. Rhonda L., Tony E., and Roger G. will be on vacation on 7/31,
IV. Andy R., Jane B., and Ethel R. will be on vacation on 7/28.

THE CORRECT ANSWER IS:

A. I, II, III   B. I, II
C. II, III   D. II

6. How many typists will be working on July 28?

    A. One   B. Two   C. Three   D. Four

7. How many computer operators will be working on July 23?

    A. One   B. Two   C. Three   D. Four

8. Roger G. will begin his vacation on July

    A. 21   B. 22   C. 23   D. 24

Questions 9-15.

DIRECTIONS: Questions 9 through 15 are to be answered on the basis of the following information.

Assume that you are the supervisor of a unit that works seven days a week. You need to determine the work and vacation schedules of the employees you supervise for the month of August.

THE EMPLOYEES

	Years Seniority	Position
Robert L.	7	Security staff
Ann N.	7 1/2	Computer operator
Thomas B.	9	Typist
Phyllis P.	11	Computer operator
Mike D.	3	Security staff
Jane R.	2	Security staff
Alan R.	8	Computer operator
Susan T.	10	Typist
George W.	6	Computer operator
Barbara L.	4	Typist
Jack B.	13	Security staff
Grace N.	12	Typist

THE VACATION PREFERENCES OF THE EMPLOYEES

	1st vacation day	last vacation day
Robert L.	8/3	8/18
Ann N.	8/17	8/28
Thomas B.	8/19	8/28
Phyllis P.	8/5	8/20
Mike D.	8/14	8/21
Jane R.	8/20	8/27
Alan R.	8/12	8/26
Susan T.	8/5	8/26
George W.	8/3	8/14
Barbara L.	8/7	8/21
Jack B.	8/10	8/18
Grace N.	8/4	8/25

IMPORTANT REGULATIONS REGARDING VACATION LEAVE.

Employees with seniority have first choice for their preferred vacation dates. Seniority should be calculated separately for each of the three occupational groups.

There must be two security employees on duty each working day in August. This overrides any other considerations.

There must be two typists on duty from 8/11 to 8/18. This overrides any other considerations.

There must be two computer operators on duty each working day in August. This overrides any other considerations.

Employees with least seniority, when denied their first choice of vacation dates, should automatically be scheduled ahead for their vacation on the very next date closest to the date they originally preferred, and the length of the vacation extended the appropriate number of days. Example: A vacation originally requested for 8/18, but changed because of seniority, would be moved AHEAD to a date after 8/18 (to 8/21, for example).

You may wish to use the calendar on the next page to help you organize this information.

AUGUST

1	2	3	4	5	6	7
8	9	10	11	12	13	14
15	16	17	18	19	20	21
22	23	24	25	26	27	28
29	30	31				

9. How many workers will be on vacation on August 21? 9._____
   A. Five B. Six C. Seven D. Eight

10. How many workers will be working on August 28? 10._____
    A. Six B. Seven C. Eight D. Nine

11. Of the following, who will NOT work on August 27? 11._____
    A. Alan R.   B. George W.   C. Mike D.   D. Susan T.

12. Of the following, who will work on August 19? 12._____
    A. Thomas B.   B. Barbara L.
    C. Ann N.   D. Mike D.

13. How many typists will be on vacation on August 19? 13._____
    A. One   B. Two   C. Three   D. Four

14. How many workers will be on vacation on August 17? 14._____
    A. Five   B. Six   C. Eight   D. Nine

15. How many workers will work on August 11? 15._____
    A. Seven   B. Eight   C. Five   D. Six

KEY (CORRECT ANSWERS)

1. C	6. B	11. B
2. B	7. A	12. C
3. A	8. C	13. D
4. B	9. D	14. B
5. C	10. C	15. A

EXAMINATION SECTION
TEST 1

DIRECTIONS: Each question or incomplete statement is followed by several suggested answers or completions. Select the one that BEST answers the question or completes the statement. *PRINT THE LETTER OF THE CORRECT ANSWER IN THE SPACE AT THE RIGHT.*

1. Which of the following is the MOST likely action a supervisor should take to help establish an effective working relationship with his departmental superiors? 1.____
    A. Delay the implementation of new procedures received from superiors in order to evaluate their appropriateness.
    B. Skip the chain of command whenever he feels that it is to his advantage
    C. Keep supervisors informed of problems in his area and the steps taken to correct them
    D. Don't take up superiors' time by discussing anticipated problems but wait until the difficulties occur

2. Of the following, the action a supervisor could take which would generally be MOST conducive to the establishment of an effective working relationship with employees includes 2.____
    A. maintaining impersonal relationships to prevent development of biased actions
    B. treating all employees equally without adjusting for individual differences
    C. continuous observation of employees on the job with insistence on constant improvement
    D. careful planning and scheduling of work for your employees

3. Which of the following procedures is the LEAST likely to establish effective working relationships between employees and supervisors? 3.____
    A. Encouraging two-way communication with employees
    B. Periodic discussion with employees regarding their job performance
    C. Ignoring employees' gripes concerning job difficulties
    D. Avoiding personal prejudices in dealing with employees

4. Criticism can be used as a tool to point out the weak areas of a subordinate's work performance.
   Of the following, the BEST action for a supervisor to take so that his criticism will be accepted is to 4.____
    A. focus his criticism on the act instead of on the person
    B. exaggerate the errors in order to motivate the employee to do better
    C. pass judgment quickly and privately without investigating the circumstances of the error
    D. generalize the criticism and not specifically point out the errors in performance

5. In trying to improve the motivation of his subordinates, a supervisor can achieve the BEST results by taking action based upon the assumption that most employees
   A. have an inherent dislike of work
   B. wish to be closely directed
   C. are more interested in security than in assuming responsibility
   D. will exercise self-direction without coercion

6. When there are conflicts or tensions between top management and lower-level employees in any department, the supervisor should FIRST attempt to
   A. represent and enforce the management point of view
   B. act as the representative of the workers to get their ideas across to management
   C. serve as a two-way spokesman, trying to interpret each side to the other
   D. remain neutral, but keep informed of changes in the situation

7. A probationary period for new employees is usually provided in many agencies. The MAJOR purpose of such a period is usually to
   A. allow a determination of employee's suitability for the position
   B. obtain evidence as to employee's ability to perform in a higher position
   C. conform to requirements that ethnic hiring goals be met for all positions
   D. train the new employee in the duties of the position

8. An effective program of orientation for new employees usually includes all of the following EXCEPT
   A. having the supervisor introduce the new employee to his job, outlining his responsibilities and how to carry them out
   B. permitting the new worker to tour the facility or department so he can observe all parts of it in action
   C. scheduling meetings for new employees, at which the job requirements are explained to them and they are given personnel manuals
   D. testing the new worker on his skills and sending him to a centralized in-service workshop

9. In-service training is an important responsibility of many supervisors. The MAJOR reason for such training is to
   A. avoid future grievance procedures because employees might say they were not prepared to carry out their jobs
   B. maximize the effectiveness of the department by helping each employee perform at his full potential
   C. satisfy inspection teams from central headquarters of the department
   D. help prevent disagreements with members of the community

10. There are many forms of useful in-service training. Of the following, the training method which is NOT an appropriate technique for leadership development is to
    A. provide special workshops or clinics in activity skills
    B. conduct institutes to familiarize new workers with the program of the department and with their roles

C. schedule team meetings for problem-solving, including both supervisors and leaders
D. have the leader rate himself on an evaluation form periodically

11. Of the following techniques of evaluating work training programs, the one that is BEST is to
    A. pass out a carefully designed questionnaire to the trainees at the completion of the program
    B. test the knowledge that trainees have both at the beginning of training and at its completion
    C. interview the trainees at the completion of the program
    D. evaluate performance before and after training for both a control group and an experimental group

12. Assume that a new supervisor is having difficulty making his instructions to subordinates clearly understood.
    The one of the following which is the FIRST step he should take in dealing with this problem is to
    A. set up a training workshop in communication skills
    B. determine the extent and nature of the communications gap
    C. repeat both verbal and written instructions several times
    D. simplify his written and spoken vocabulary

13. A director has not properly carried out the orders of his assistant supervisor on several occasions to the point where he has been successively warned, reprimanded, and severely reprimanded.
    When the director once again does not carry out orders, the PROPER action for the assistant supervisor to take is to
    A. bring the director up on charges of failing to perform his duties properly
    B. have a serious discussion with the director, explaining the need for the orders and the necessity for carrying them out
    C. recommend that the director be transferred to another district
    D. severely reprimand the director again, making clear that no further deviation will be countenanced

14. A supervisor with several subordinates becomes aware that two of these subordinates are neither friendly nor congenial.
    In making assignments, it would be BEST for the supervisor to
    A. disregard the situation
    B. disregard the situation in making a choice of assignment but emphasize the need for teamwork
    C. investigate the situation to find out who is at fault and give that individual the less desirable assignments until such time as he corrects his attitude
    D. place the unfriendly subordinates in positions where they have as little contact with one another as possible

15. A DESIRABLE characteristic of a good supervisor is that he should
    A. identify himself with his subordinates rather than with higher management
    B. inform subordinates of forthcoming changes in policies and programs only when they directly affect the subordinates' activities
    C. make advancement of the subordinates contingent on personal loyalty to the supervisor
    D. make promises to subordinates only when sure of the ability to keep them

16. The supervisor who is MOST likely to be successful is the one who
    A. refrains from exercising the special privileges of his position
    B. maintains a formal attitude toward his subordinates
    C. maintains an informal attitude toward his subordinates
    D. represents the desires of his subordinate to his superiors

17. Application of sound principles of human relations by a supervisor may be expected to _____ the need for formal discipline.
    A. decrease
    B. have no effect on
    C. increase
    D. obviate

18. The MOST important generally approved way to maintain or develop high morale in one's subordinates is to
    A. give warnings and reprimands in a jocular way
    B. excuse from staff conferences those employees who are busy
    C. keep them informed of new developments and policies of higher management
    D. refrain from criticizing their faults directly

19. In training subordinates, an IMPORTANT principle for the supervisor to recognize is that
    A. a particular method of instruction will be of substantially equal value for all employees in a given title
    B. it is difficult to train people over 50 years of age because they have little capacity for learning
    C. persons undergoing the same course of training will learn at different rates of speed
    D. training can seldom achieve its purpose unless individual instruction is the chief method used

20. Over an extended period of time, a subordinate is MOST likely to become and remain most productive if the supervisor
    A. accords praise to the subordinate whenever his work is satisfactory, withholding criticism except in the case of very inferior work
    B. avoids both praise and criticism except for outstandingly good or bad work performed by the subordinate
    C. informs the subordinate of his shortcomings, as viewed by management, while according praise only when highly deserved
    D. keeps the subordinate informed of the degree of satisfaction with which his performance of the job is viewed by management.

KEY (CORRECT ANSWERS)

1.	C	11.	D
2.	D	12.	B
3.	C	13.	A
4.	A	14.	D
5.	D	15.	D
6.	C	16.	D
7.	A	17.	A
8.	D	18.	C
9.	B	19.	C
10.	D	20.	D

TEST 2

DIRECTIONS: Each question or incomplete statement is followed by several suggested answers or completions. Select the one that BEST answers the question or completes the statement. *PRINT THE LETTER OF THE CORRECT ANSWER IN THE SPACE AT THE RIGHT.*

1. A supervisor has just been told by a subordinate, Mr. Jones, that another employee, Mr. Smith, deliberately disobeyed an important rule of the department by taking home some confidential departmental material.
   Of the following courses of action, it would be MOST advisable for the supervisor FIRST to
   A. discuss the matter privately with both Mr. Jones and Mrs. Smith at the same time
   B. call a meeting of the entire staff and discuss the matter generally without mentioning any employee by name
   C. arrange to supervise Mr. Smith's activities more closely
   D. discuss the matter privately with Mr. Smith

   1.____

2. The one of the following actions which would be MOST efficient and economical for a supervisor to take to minimize the effect of periodical fluctuations in the workload of his unit is to
   A. increase his permanent staff until it is large enough to handle the work of the busy loads
   B. request the purchase of time- and labor-saving equipment to be used primarily during the busy loads
   C. lower, temporarily, the standards for quality of work performance during peak loads
   D. schedule for the slow periods work that is not essential to perform during the busy periods

   2.____

3. Discipline of employees is usually a supervisor's responsibility. There may be several useful forms of disciplinary action.
   Of the following, the form that is LEAST appropriate is the
   A. written reprimand or warning
   B. involuntary transfer to another work setting
   C. demotion or suspension
   D. assignment of added hours of work each week

   3.____

4. Of the following, the MOST effective means of dealing with employee disciplinary problems is to
   A. give personality tests to individuals to identify their psychological problems
   B. distribute and discuss a policy manual containing exact rules governing employee behavior
   C. establish a single, clear penalty to be imposed for all wrongdoing irrespective of degree
   D. have supervisors get to know employees well through social mingling

   4.____

5. A recently developed technique for appraising work performance is to have the supervisor record on a continual basis all significant incidents in each subordinate's behavior that indicate unsuccessful action and those that indicate poor behavior.
Of the following, a MAJOR disadvantage of this method of performance appraisal is that it
   A. often leads to overly close supervision
   B. results in competition among those subordinates being evaluated
   C. tends to result in superficial judgments
   D. lacks objectivity for evaluating performance

6. Assume that you are a supervisor and have observed the performance of an employee during a period of time. You have concluded that his performance needs improvement.
In order to improve his performance, it would, therefore, be BEST for you to
   A. note your findings in the employee's personnel folder so that his behavior is a matter of record
   B. report the findings to the personnel officer so he can take prompt action
   C. schedule a problem-solving conference with the employee
   D. recommend his transfer to simpler duties

7. When an employee's absences or latenesses seem to be nearing excessiveness, the supervisor should speak with him to find out what the problem is.
Of the following, if such a discussion produces no reasonable explanation, the discussion usually BEST serves to
   A. affirm clearly the supervisor's adherence to proper policy
   B. alert other employees that such behavior is unacceptable
   C. demonstrate that the supervisor truly represents higher management
   D. notify the employee that his behavior is being observed and evaluated

8. Assume that an employee willfully and recklessly violates an important agency regulation. The nature of the violation is of such magnitude that it demands immediate action, but the facts of the case are not entirely clear. Further, assume that the supervisor is free to make any of the following recommendations.
The MOST appropriate action for the supervisor to take is to recommend that the employee be
   A. discharged   B. suspended
   C. forced to resign   D. transferred

9. Although employees' titles may be identical, each position in that title may be considerably different.
Of the following, a supervisor should carefully assign each employee to a specific position based PRIMARILY on the employee's
   A. capability   B. experience   C. education   D. seniority

10. The one of the following situations where it is MOST appropriate to transfer an employee to a similar assignment is one in which the employee
    A. lacks motivation and interest
    B. experiences a personality conflict with his supervisor
    C. is negligent in the performance of his duties
    D. lacks capacity or ability to perform assigned tasks

10.____

11. The one of the following which is LEAST likely to be affected by improvements in the morale of personnel is employee
    A. skill
    B. absenteeism
    C. turnover
    D. job satisfaction

11.____

12. The one of the following situations in which it is LEAST appropriate for a supervisor to delegate authority to subordinates is where the supervisor
    A. lacks confidence in his own abilities to perform certain work
    B. is overburdened and cannot handle all his responsibilities
    C. refers all disciplinary problems to his subordinate
    D. has to deal with an emergency or crisis

12.____

13. Assume that it has come to your attention that two of your subordinates have shouted at each other and have almost engaged in a fist fight. Luckily, they were separated by some of the other employees.
    Of the following, your BEST immediate course of action would generally be to
    A. reprimand the senior of the two subordinates since he should have known better
    B. hear the story from both employees and any witnesses and then take needed disciplinary action
    C. ignore the matter since nobody was physically hurt
    D. immediately suspend and fine both employees pending a departmental hearing

13.____

14. You have been delegating some of your authority to one of your subordinates because of his leadership potential.
    Which of the following actions is LEAST conducive to the growth and development of this individual for a supervisory position?
    A. Use praise only when it will be effective
    B. Give very detailed instructions and supervise the employee closely to be sure that the instructions ae followed precisely
    C. Let the subordinate proceed with his planned course of action even if mistakes, within a permissible range, are made
    D. Intervene on behalf of the subordinate whenever an assignment becomes difficult for him

14.____

15. A rumor has been spreading in your department concerning the possibility of layoffs due to decreased revenues.
    As a supervisor, you should GENERALLY
    A. deny the rumor, whether it is true or false, in order to keep morale from declining

15.____

B. inform the men to the best of your knowledge about this situation and keep them advised of any new information
C. tell the men to forget about the rumor and concentrate on increasing their productivity
D. ignore the rumor since it is not authorized information

16. Within an organization, every supervisor should know to whom he reports and who reports to him.
The one of the following which is achieved by use of such structured relationships is
    A. unity of command
    B. confidentiality
    C. esprit de corps
    D. promotion opportunities

16.____

17. Almost every afternoon, one of your employees comes back from his break ten minutes late without giving you any explanation.
Which of the following actions should you take FIRST in this situation?
    A. Assign the employee to a different type of work and observe whether his behavior changes
    B. Give the employee extra work to do so that he will have to return on time
    C. Ask the employee for an explanation for his lateness
    D. Tell the employee he is jeopardizing the break for everyone

17.____

18. When giving instructions to your employees in a group, which one of the following should you make certain to do?
    A. Speak in a casual, off-hand manner
    B. Assume that your employees fully understand the instructions
    C. Write out your instructions beforehand and read them to the employees
    D. Tell exactly who is to do what

18.____

19. A fist fight develops between two men under your supervision.
The MOST advisable course of action for you to take FIRST is to
    A. call the police
    B. have the other workers pull them apart
    C. order them to stop
    D. step between the two men

19.____

20. You have assigned some difficult and unusual work to one of your most experienced and competent subordinates.
If you notice that he is doing the work incorrectly, you should
    A. assign the work to another employee
    B. reprimand him in private
    C. show him immediately how the work should be done
    D. wait until the job is completed and then correct his errors

20.____

KEY (CORRECT ANSWERS)

1.	D	11.	A
2.	D	12.	C
3.	D	13.	B
4.	B	14.	B
5.	A	15.	B
6.	C	16.	A
7.	D	17.	C
8.	B	18.	D
9.	A	19.	C
10.	B	20.	C

EXAMINATION SECTION
TEST 1

DIRECTIONS: Each question or incomplete statement is followed by several suggested answers or completions. Select the one that BEST answers the question or completes the statement. *PRINT THE LETTER OF THE CORRECT ANSWER IN THE SPACE AT THE RIGHT.*

1. A supervisor was given a booklet that showed a new work method that could save time. He didn't tell his men because he thought that they would get the booklet anyway.
   For the supervisor to have acted like this is a
   A. *good* idea, because he saves time and both of talking to the men
   B. *bad* idea, because he should make sure his men know about better work methods
   C. *good* idea, because the men would rather read about it themselves
   D *bad* idea, because a supervisor should always show his men every memo he gets from higher authority

1.____

2. A supervisor found it necessary to discipline two subordinates. One man had been operating his equipment in a wrong way, while the other man came to work late for three days in a row. The supervisor decided to talk to both men together.
   For the supervisor to deal with the problems in this way is a
   A. *good* idea because each man will learn about the difficulties of the other person and how to solve such difficulties
   B. *bad* idea because the supervisor should wait until he can bring a larger group together and save time in discussing such questions
   C. *good* idea because he will be able to get the men to see that their problems are related
   D. *bad* idea because he should meet with each man separately and give him his full attention

2.____

3. A supervisor should try to make his men feel their jobs are important in order to
   A. get the men to say good things about their supervisor to his own superior
   B. get the men to think in terms of advancing to better jobs
   C. let higher management in the agency know that the supervisor is efficient
   D. help the men to be able to work more efficiently and enthusiastically

3.____

4. A supervisor should know approximately how long it takes to do a particular kind of job CHIEFLY because he
   A. will know how much time to take if he has to do it himself
   B. will be able to tell his men to do it even faster
   C. can judge the performance of the person doing the job
   D. can retrain experienced employees in better work habits

4.____

5. Supervisors often get their employees' opinions about better work methods because
    A. the men will know that they are respected
    B. the men would otherwise lose all their confidence in the supervisor
    C. the supervisor might find in this way a good suggestion he could use
    D. this is the best method for improvement of work methods

6. Right after you have trained your subordinates in doing a new job, you find that they seem to be doing all right, but that it will take them several days to finish. You also have several groups of men working at other locations.
    The MOST efficient way for you to make sure that the men continue doing the new job properly is to
    A. stay on that job with the men until it is finished just in case trouble develops
    B. visit the men every half hour until the job is done
    C. stay away from their job that day and visit the men the next day to ask them if they had any problems
    D. visit the men a few times each day until they finish the new job

7. Assume that one of your new employees is older than you are. You also think that he may be hard to get along with because he is older than you.
    The BEST way for you to avoid any problems with the older worker is for you to
    A. lay down the law immediately and tell the man he better not cause you any trouble
    B. treat the man just the way you would any other worker
    C. always ask the older worker for advice in the presence of all the men
    D. ignore the man entirely until he realizes that you are the boss

8. Assume that you have tried a new method suggested by one of your employees and find that it is easier and cheaper than the method you had been using.
    The PROPER thing for you to do NEXT is to
    A. say nothing to anyone but train your men to use the new method
    B. train your men to use the new method and tell your crew that you got the idea from one of the men
    C. continue using the old method because a supervisor should not use suggestions of his men
    D. have your crew learn the new method and take credit for the idea since you are the boss

9. Suppose you are a supervisor and your superior tells you that the way your men are doing a certain procedure is wrong and that you should re-train our men as soon as possible.
    When you begin to re-train the men, the FIRST thing you should do is to
    A. tell your men that a wrong procedure had been used and that a new method must be learned as a result
    B. train your employees in the new method with no explanation since you are the boss

C. tell the crew that your superior has just decided that everyone should learn a new method
D. tell the crew that your superior says your method is wrong but that you don't agree with this

10. It is BAD practice to criticize a man in front of the other men because
    A. people will think you are too strict
    B. it is annoying to anyone who walks by
    C. it is embarrassing to the man concerned
    D. it will antagonize the other men

    10._____

11. A supervisor decides not to put his two best men on a work detail because he knows that they won't like it.
    For the supervisor to make the work assignment this way is a
    A. *good* idea because it is only fair to give your best men a break once in a while
    B. *bad* idea because you should treat all of your me fairly and not show favoritism
    C. *good* idea because you save the strength of these men for another job
    D. *bad* idea because more of the men should be exempted from the assignment

    11._____

12. Suppose you are a supervisor and you find it inconvenient to obey an established procedure set by your agency. You think another procedure would be better.
    The BEST thing to do first about this procedure that you don't like is for you to
    A. obey the procedure even if you don't to and suggest your idea to your own supervisor
    B. disregard the procedure because a supervisor is supposed to have some privileges
    C. follow the procedure some of the time but ignore it when the men are not watching
    D. organize a group of other supervisors to get the procedure changed

    12._____

13. A supervisor estimated that it would take his crew one workday per week to do a certain job each week. However, after a month he noticed that the job averaged two and a half days a week and this delayed other jobs that had to be done.
    The FIRST thing that the supervisor should do in this case is to
    A. call him men together and warn them that they will get a poor work evaluation if they do not work harder
    B. talk to each man personally, asking him to work harder on the job
    C. go back and study the maintenance job by himself to see if more men should be assigned to the job
    D. write his boss a report describing in detail how much time it is taking the men to do the job

    13._____

14. An employee complains to you that some of the work assignments are too difficult to do alone.
Which of the following is the BEST way for you to handle this complaint?
    A. Go with him to see exactly what he does and why he finds it so difficult
    B. Politely tell the man that he has to do the job or be brought up on charges
    C. Tell the man to send his complaint to the head of your agency
    D. Sympathize with the man and give him easier jobs

14.____

15. The BEST way for a supervisor to keep control of his work assignments is to
    A. ask the men to report to him immediately when their jobs are finished
    B. walk around the buildings once a week and get a first-hand view of what is being done
    C. keep his ears open for problems and complaints, but leave the men aloe to do the work
    D. write up a work schedule and check it periodically against the actual work done

15.____

16. A supervisor made a work schedule for his men. At the bottom of it, he wrote, *No changes or exceptions will be made in this schedule for any reason.*
For the supervisor to have made this statement is
    A. *good*, because the men will respect the supervisor for his attitude
    B. *bad*, because there are emergencies and special situations that occur
    C. *good*, because each man will know exactly what is expected of him
    D. *bad*, because the men should expect that no changes will ever be made in the work schedule without written permission

16.____

17. Which one of the following would NOT be a result of a well-planned work schedule?
The schedule
    A. makes efficient use of the time of the staff
    B. acts as a checklist for an important job that might be left out
    C. will give an idea of the work to a substitute supervisor
    D. shows at a glance who the best men are

17.____

18. A new piece of equipment you have ordered is delivered. You are familiar with it, but the men under you who will use it do not know the equipment.
Of the following methods, which is the BEST to take in explaining to them how to operate this equipment?
    A. Ask the men to watch other crews using the equipment
    B. Show one reliable man how to operate the equipment and ask him to teach the other men
    C. Ask the men to read the instructions in the manual for the equipment
    D. Call the men together and show them how to operate the equipment

18.____

19. One supervisor assigns work to his men by calling his crew together each week and describing what has to be done that week. He then tells them to arrange individual assignments among themselves and to work as a team during the week.

19.____

This method of scheduling work is a
- A. *good* idea because this guarantees that the men will work together
- B. *bad* idea because responsibility for doing the job is poorly fixed
- C. *good* idea because the men will finish the job in less time, working together
- D. *bad* idea because the supervisor should always stay with his men

20. Suppose that an employee came to his supervisor with a problem concerning his assignment.
For the supervisor to listen to his problem is a
- A. *good* idea because a supervisor should always take time off to talk when one of his men wants to talk
- B. *bad* idea because the supervisor should not be bothered during the work day
- C. *good* idea because it is the job of the supervisor to deal with problems of job assignment
- D. *bad* idea because the employee could start annoying the supervisor with all sorts of problems

20.____

21. Suppose that on the previous afternoon you were looking for an experienced employee in order to give him an emergency job and he was missing from his job location. The next morning, he tells you that he got sick suddenly and had to go home, but could not tell you since you were not around. He has never done this before.
What should you do?
- A. Tell the man he is excused and that in such circumstances he did the wisest thing
- B. Bring the man up on charges because whatever he says he could still have notified you
- C. Have the man examined by a doctor to see if he really was sick the day before
- D. Explain to the mean that he should make every effort to tell you or to get a message to you if he must leave

21.____

22. An employee had a grievance and went to his supervisor about it. The employee was not satisfied with the way the supervisor tried to help him and told him so. Yet, the supervisor had done everything he could under the circumstances.
The PROPER action for the supervisor to take at this time is to
- A. politely tell the employee that there is nothing more for the supervisor to do about the problem
- B. let the employee know how he can bring his complaint to a higher authority
- C. tell the employee that he must solve the problem on his own since he did not want to follow the supervisor's advice
- D. suggest to the employee that he ask for another supervisor for assistance

22.____

23. In which of the following situations is it BEST to give your men spoken rather than written orders?
    A. You want your men to have a record of the instructions.
    B. Spoken instructions are less likely to be forgotten.
    C. An emergency situation has arisen in which there is no time to write up instructions.
    D. There are instructions on time and leave regulations which are complicated.

24. One of your employees tells you that a week ago he had a small accident on the job but he did not bother telling you because he was able to continue working.
    For the employee not to have told his supervisor about the accident was
    A. *good*, because the accident was a small one
    B. *bad*, because all accidents should be reported, no matter how small
    C. *good*, because the supervisor should be bothered only for important matters
    D. *bad*, because having an accident is one way to get excused for the day

25. For a supervisor to deal with each of his subordinate in exactly the same manner is
    A. *poor*, because each man presents a different problem and there is no one way of handling all problems
    B. *good*, because once a problem is handled with one man, he can handle another man with the same problem
    C. *poor*, because the men will resent it if they are not handled each in a better way than others
    D. *good*, because this assures fair and impartial treatment of each subordinate

KEY (CORRECT ANSWERS)

1. B
2. D
3. D
4. C
5. C

6. D
7. B
8. B
9. A
10. C

11. B
12. A
13. C
14. A
15. D

16. B
17. D
18. D
19. B
20. C

21. D
22. B
23. C
24. B
25. A

TEST 2

DIRECTIONS: Each question or incomplete statement is followed by several suggested answers or completions. Select the one that BEST answers the question or completes the statement. *PRINT THE LETTER OF THE CORRECT ANSWER IN THE SPACE AT THE RIGHT.*

1. Jim Johnson has been on your staff for over four years. He has always been a conscientious and productive worker. About a month ago, his wife died; and since that time, his work performance has been very poor.
   As his supervisor, which one of the following is the BEST way for you to deal with this situation?
   A. Allow Jim as much time as he needs to overcome his grief and hope that his work performance improves
   B. Meet with Jim to discuss ways to improve his performance
   C. Tell Jim directly that you are more concerned with his work performance than with his personal problem
   D. Prepare disciplinary action on Jim as soon as possible

    1.____

2. You are responsible for the overall operation of a storehouse which is divided into two sections. Each section has its own supervisor. You have decided to make several complex changes in the storekeeping procedures which will affect both sections.
   Of the following, the BEST way to make sure that these changes are understood by the two supervisors is for you to
   A. meet with both supervisors to discuss the changes
   B. issue a memorandum to each supervisor explaining the changes
   C. post the changes where the supervisors are sure to see them
   D. instruct one supervisor to explain the changes to the other supervisor

    2.____

3. You have called a meeting of all your subordinates to tell them what has to be done on a new project in which they will all be involved. Several times during the meeting, you ask if there are any questions about what you have told them.
   Of the following, to ask the subordinates whether there are any questions during the meeting can BEST be described as
   A. *inadvisable*, because it interferes with their learning about the new project
   B. *advisable*, because you will find out what they don't understand and have a chance to clear up any problems they may have
   C. *inadvisable*, because it makes the meeting too long and causes the subordinates to lose interest in the new project
   D. *advisable*, because it gives you a chance to learn which of your subordinates are paying attention to what you say

    3.____

4. As a supervisor, you are responsible for seeing to it that absenteeism does not become a problem among your subordinates.
   Which one of the following is NOT an acceptable way of controlling the problem of excessive absences?

    4.____

A. Distribute a written statement to your staff on the policies regarding absenteeism in your organization
B. Arrange for workers who have the fewest absences to talk to those workers who have the most absences
C. Let your subordinates know that a record is being kept of all absences
D. Arrange for counseling of those employees who are frequently absent

5. One of your supervisors has been an excellent worker for the past two years. There are no promotion opportunities for this worker in the foreseeable future. Due to the city's present budget crisis, a salary increase is not possible.
Under the circumstances, which one of the following actions on your part would be MOST likely to continue to motivate this worker?
   A. Tell the worker that times are bad all over and jobs are hard to find
   B. Give the worker less work and easier assignments
   C. Tell the worker to try to look for a better paying job elsewhere
   D. Seek the worker's advice often and show that the suggestions provided are appreciated

6. As a supervisor in a warehouse, it is important that you use your available work force to its fullest potential.
Which one of the following actions on your part is MOST likely to increase the effectiveness of your work force?
   A. Assigning more workers to a job than the number actually needed
   B. Eliminating all job training to allow more time for work output
   C. Using your best workers on jobs that average workers can do
   D. Making sure that all materials and equipment used are maintained in good working order

7. You learn that your storage area will soon be undergoing changes which will affect the work of your subordinates. You decide not to tell your subordinates about what is to happen.
Of the following, your action can BEST be described as
   A. *wise*, because your subordinates will learn of the changes for themselves
   B. *unwise*, because your subordinates should be advised about what is to happen
   C. *wise*, because it is better for your subordinates to continue working without being disturbed by such news
   D. *unwise*, because the work of your subordinates will gradually slow down

8. In making plans for the operation of your unit, you are MOST likely to see these plans carried out successfully if you
   A. allow your staff to participate in developing these plans
   B. do not spend any time on the minor details of these plans
   C. base these plans on the past experiences of others
   D. allow these plans to interact with outside activities in other units

9. As a supervisor in charge of the total operation of a food supply warehouse, you find vandalism to be a potentially serious problem. On occasion, trespassers have gained entrance into the facility by climbing over an unprotected 8-foot fence surrounding the warehouse whose dimensions measure 100 feet by 100 feet.
Assuming that all of the following would be equally effective ways in preventing these breaches in security in the situation described above, which one would be LEAST costly?
   A. Using two trained guard dogs to roam freely throughout the facility at night
   B. Hiring a security guard to patrol the facility after working hours
   C. Installing tape razor wire on top of the fence surrounding the facility
   D. Installing an electronic burglar alarm system requiring the installation of a new fence

10. The area for which you have program responsibility has undergone recent changes. Your staff is now required to perform many new tasks, and morale is low.
The LEAST effective way for you to improve long-term staff morale would be to
   A. develop support groups to discuss problems
   B. involve staff in job development
   C. maintain a comfortable social environment within the group
   D. adequately plan and give assignments in a timely manner

11. As a supervisor in a large office, one of your subordinate supervisors stops you in the middle of the office and complains loudly that he is being treated unfairly. The rest of the staff ceases work and listens to the complaint.
The MOST appropriate action for you to take in this situation is to
   A. ignore this unprofessional behavior and continue on your way
   B. tell the supervisor that his behavior is unprofessional and he should learn how to conduct himself
   C. explain to the supervisor why you believe he is not being treated unfairly
   D. ask the supervisor to come to your office at a specific time to discuss the matter

12. You are told that one of your subordinates is distributing literature which attempts to recruit individuals to join a particular organization. Several workers complain that their rights are being violated.
Of the following, the BEST action for you to take FIRST is to
   A. ignore the situation because no harm is being done
   B. discuss the matter further with your supervisor
   C. ask the worker to stop distributing the literature
   D. tell the workers that they do not have to read the material

13. You have been assigned to develop a short training course for a recently issued procedure.
In designing this course, which of the following statements is the LEAST important for you to consider?

A. The learning experience must be interesting and meaningful in terms of the staff member's job.
B. The method of teaching must be strictly followed in order to develop successful learning experiences.
C. The course content should incorporate the rules and regulations of the agency.
D. The procedure should be consistent with the agency's objectives.

14. As a supervisor, there are several newly-promoted employees under your supervision. Each of these employees is subject to a probationary period PRIMARILY to
    A. assess the employee's performance to see if the employee should be retained or removed from the position
    B. give the employee the option to return to his former employment if the employee is unhappy in the new position
    C. give the employee an opportunity to learn the duties and responsibilities of the position
    D. judge the employee's potential for upward mobility in the future

15. An employee under your supervision rushes into your office to tell you he has just received a telephone bomb threat.
    As the administrative supervisor, the FIRST thing you should do is
    A. evacuate staff from the floor
    B. call the police and building security
    C. advise your administrator
    D. do a preliminary search

16. After reviewing the Absence Control form for a unit under your supervision, you find that one of your staff members has a fifth undocumented sick leave within a six-month period.
    In this situation, the FIRST action you should take is to
    A. discuss the seriousness of the matter with the staff member when he returns to work and fully document the details of the discussion
    B. review the case with the location director and warn the staff member that future use of sick leave will be punished
    C. submit the proper disciplinary forms to ensure that the staff member is penalized for excessive absences
    D. request that the timekeeper put the staff member on doctor's note restriction

17. A subordinate supervisor recently assigned to your office begins his first conference with you by saying that he has learned something that another supervisor is doing that you should know about.
    After hearing this statement, of the following, the BEST approach for you to take is to
    A. explain to the supervisor that the conference is to discuss his work and not that of his co-workers
    B. tell the supervisor that you do not encourage a spy system among the staff you supervise

5 (#2)

   C. tell the supervisor that you will listen to his report only if the other supervisor is present
   D. allow the supervisor to continue talking until you have enough information to make a decision on how best to respond

18. Assume that you are a supervisor recently assigned to a new unit. You notice that, for the past few days, one of the employees in your unit whose work is about average has been stopping work at about four o'clock and has been spending the rest of the afternoon relaxing at his desk.
    The BEST of the following actions for you to take in this situation is to
    A. assign more work to this employee since it is apparent that he does not have enough work to keep him busy
    B. observe the employee's conduct more closely for about ten days before taking any more positive action
    C. discuss the matter with the employee, pointing out to him how he can use the extra hour daily to raise the level of his job performance
    D. question the previous supervisor in charge of the unit in order to determine whether he had sanctioned such conduct when he supervised that unit

18.____

19. A new supervisor was assigned to your program four months ago. Although he tries hard, he has been unable to meet certain standards because he still has a lot to learn. As his supervisor, you are required to submit performance evaluations within a few days.
    How would you rate this employee on the tasks where he fails to meet standards because of lack of experience?
    A. Satisfactory   B. Conditional
    C. Unsatisfactory   D. Unratable

19.____

20. You find that there is an important procedural error in a memo which you distributed to your staff several days ago.
    The BEST approach for you to take at this time is to
    A. send a corrected memo to the staff, indicating what prior error was made
    B. send a corrected memo to the staff without mentioning the prior error
    C. tell the staff about the error at the next monthly staff meeting
    D. place the corrected memo on the office bulletin board

20.____

21. Your superior asks you, a supervisor, about the status of the response to a letter from a public official concerning a client's case. When you ask the subordinate who was assigned to prepare the response to give you the letter, the subordinate denies that it was given to him. You are certain that the subordinate has the letter, but is withholding it because the response has not yet been prepared.
    Of the following, in order to secure the letter from the subordinate, you should FIRST
    A. accuse the subordinate of lying and demand that the letter be given to you immediately
    B. say that you would consider it a personal favor if the subordinate would find the letter

21.____

C. continue to question the subordinate until he admits to having been given the letter
D. offer a face-saving solution, such as asking the subordinate to look again for the letter

22. As a supervisor, you have been assigned to write a few paragraphs to be included in the agency's annual report, describing a public service agency department this year as compared to last year.
Which of the following elements basic to the agency is LEAST likely to have changed since last year?
A. Mission   B. Structure   C. Technology   D. Personnel

23. As a supervisor, you have been informed that a grievance has been filed against you, accusing you of assigning a subordinate to out-of-title tasks.
Of the following, the BEST approach for you to take is to
A. waive the grievance so that it will proceed to a Step II hearing
B. immediately change the subordinate's assignment to avoid future problems
C. respond to the grievance, giving appropriate reasons for the assignment
D. review the job description to ensure that the subordinate's tasks are not out-of-title

24. Which of the following is NOT a correct statement about agency group training programs in a public service agency?
A. Training sessions continue for an indefinite period of time.
B. Group training sessions are planned for designated personnel.
C. Training groups are organized formally through administrative planning.
D. Group training is task-centered and aimed toward accomplishing specific educational goals.

25. As a supervisor, you have submitted a memo to your superior requesting a conference to discuss the performance of a manager under your supervision. The memo states that the manager has a good working relationship with her staff; however, she tends to interpret agency policy too liberally and shows poor administrative skills by missing some deadlines and not keeping proper controls.
Which of the following steps should NOT be taken in order to prepare for this conference with your superior?
A. Collect and review all your notes regarding the manager's prior performance.
B. Outline your agenda so that you will have sufficient time to discuss the situation.
C. Tell the manager that you will be discussing her performance with your superior.
D. Clearly define objectives which will focus on improving the manager's performance.

KEY (CORRECT ANSWERS)

1.	B	11.	D
2.	A	12.	C
3.	B	13.	B
4.	B	14.	A
5.	D	15.	B
6.	D	16.	A
7.	B	17.	D
8.	A	18.	C
9.	C	19.	B
10.	C	20.	A

21. D
22. A
23. C
24. A
25. C

SUPERVISION STUDY GUIDE

Social science has developed information about groups and leadership in general and supervisor-employee relationships in particular. Since organizational effectiveness is closely linked to the ability of supervisors to direct the activities of employees, these findings are important to executives everywhere.

IS A SUPERVISOR A LEADER?

First-line supervisors are found in all large business and government organizations. They are the men at the base of an organizational hierarchy. Decisions made by the head of the organization reach them through a network of intermediate positions. They are frequently referred to as part of the management team, but their duties seldom seem to support this description.

A supervisor of clerks, tax collectors, meat inspectors, or securities analysts is not charged with budget preparation. He cannot hire or fire the employees in his own unit on his say-so. He does not administer programs which require great planning, coordinating, or decision making.

Then what is he? He is the man who is directly in charge of a group of employees doing productive work for a business or government agency. If the work requires the use of machines, the men he supervises operate them. If the work requires the writing of reports, the men he supervises write them. He is expected to maintain a productive flow of work without creating problems which higher levels of management must solve. But is he a leader?

To carry out a specific part of an agency's mission, management creates a unit, staffs it with a group of employees and designates a supervisor to take charge of them. Management directs what this unit shall do, from time to time changes directions, and often indicates what the group should not do. Management presumably creates status for the supervisor by giving him more pay, a title, and special privileges.

Management asks a supervisor to get his workers to attain organizational goals, including the desired quantity and quality of production. Supposedly, he has authority to enable him to achieve this objective. Management at least assumes that by establishing the status of the supervisor's position, it has created sufficient authority to enable him to achieve these goals—not his goals, nor necessarily the group's, but management's goals.

In addition, supervision includes writing reports, keeping records of membership in a higher-level administrative group, industrial engineering, safety engineering, editorial duties, housekeeping duties, etc. The supervisor as a member of an organizational network, must be responsible to the changing demands of the management above him. At the same time, he must be responsive to the demands of the work group of which he is a member. He is placed in the difficult position of communicating and implementing new decisions, changed programs and revised production quotas for his work group, although he may have had little part in developing them.

It follows, then, that supervision has a special characteristic: achievement of goals, previously set by management, through the efforts of others. It is in this feature of the supervisor's job that we find the role of a leader in the sense of the following definition: *A leader is that person who <u>most</u> effectively influences group activities toward goal setting and goal achievements.*

This definition is broad. It covers both leaders in groups that come together voluntarily and in those brought together through a work assignment in a factory, store, or government agency. In the natural group, the authority necessary to attain goals is determined by the group membership and is granted by them. In the working group, it is apparent that the establishment of a supervisory position creates a predisposition on the part of employees to accept the authority of the occupant of that position. We cannot, however, assume that mere occupation confers authority sufficient to assure the accomplishment of an organization's goals.

Supervision is different, then, from leadership. The supervisor is expected to fulfill the role of leader but without obtaining a grant of authority from the group he supervises. The supervisor is expected to influence the group in the achieving of goals but is often handicapped by having little influence on the organizational process by which goals are set. The supervisor, because he works in an organizational setting, has the burdens of additional organizational duties and restrictions and requirements arising out of the fact that his position is subordinate to a hierarchy of higher-level supervisors. These differences between leadership and supervision are reflected in our definition: *Supervision is basically a leadership role, in a formal organization, which has as its objective the effective influencing of other employees.*

Even though these differences between supervision and leadership exist, a significant finding of experimenters in this field is that supervisors <u>must</u> be leaders to be successful.

The problem is: How can a supervisor exercise leadership in an organizational setting? We might say that the supervisor is expected to be a natural leader in a situation which does not come about naturally. His situation becomes really difficult in an organization which is more eager to make its supervisors into followers rather than leaders.

LEADERSHIP: NATURAL AND ORGANIZATIONAL

Leadership, in its usual sense of *natural* leadership, and supervision are not the same. In some cases, leadership embraces broader powers and functions than supervision; in other cases, supervision embraces more than leadership. This is true both because of the organization and technical aspects of the supervisor's job and because of the relatively freer setting and inherent authority of the natural leader.

The natural leader usually has much more authority and influence than the supervisor. Group members not only follow his command but prefer it that way. The employee, however, can appeal the supervisor's commands to his union or to the supervisor's superior or to the personnel office. These intercessors represent restrictions on the supervisor's power to lead.

The natural leader can gain greater membership involvement in the group's objectives, and he can change the objectives of the group. The supervisor can attempt to gain employee support only for management's objectives; he cannot set other objectives. In these instances leadership is broader than supervision.

The natural leader must depend upon whatever skills are available when seeking to attain objectives. The supervisor is trained in the administrative skills necessary to achieve management's goals. If he does not possess the requisite skills, however, he can call upon management's technicians.

A natural leader can maintain his leadership, in certain groups, merely by satisfying members' need for group affiliation. The supervisor must maintain his leadership by directing and organizing his group to achieve specific organizational goals set for him and his group by management. He must have a technical competence and a kind of coordinating ability which is not needed by many natural leaders.

A natural leader is responsible only to his group which grants him authority. The supervisor is responsible to management, which employs him, and also to the work group of which he is a member. The supervisor has the exceedingly difficult job of reconciling the demands of two groups frequently in conflict. He is often placed in the untenable position of trying to play two antagonistic roles. In the above instance, supervision is broader than leadership.

ORGANIZATIONAL INFLUENCES ON LEADERSHIP

The supervisor is both a product and a prisoner of the organization wherein we find him. The organization which creates the supervisor's position also obstructs, restricts, and channelizes the exercise of his duties. These influences extend beyond prescribed functional relationships to specific supervisory behavior. For example, even in a face-to-face situation involving one of his subordinates, the supervisor's actions are controlled to a great extent by his organization. His behavior must conform to the organization policy on human relations, rules which dictate personnel procedures, specific prohibitions governing conduct, the attitudes of his own superior, etc. He is not a free agent operating within the limits of his work group. His freedom of action is much more circumscribed than is generally admitted. The organizational influences which limit his leadership actions can be classified as structure, prescriptions, and proscriptions.

The organizational structure places each supervisor's position in context with other designated positions. It determines the relationships between his position and specific positions which impinge on his. The structure of the organization designates a certain position to which he looks for orders and information about his work. It gives a particular status to his position within a pattern of statuses from which he perceives that (1) certain positions are on a par, organizationally, with his, (2) other positions are subordinate, and (3) still others are superior.

The organizational structure determines those positions to which he should look for advice and assistance, and those positions to which he should give advice and assistance.

For instance, the organizational structure has predetermined that the supervisor of a clerical processing unit shall report to a supervisory position in a higher echelon. He shall have certain relationships with the supervisors of the work units which transmit work to and receive work from his unit. He shall discuss changes and clarification of procedures with certain staff units, such as organization and methods, cost accounting, and personnel. He shall consult supervisors of units which provide or receive special work assignments.

The organizational structure, however, establishes patterns other than those of the relationships of positions. These are the patterns of responsibility, authority, and expectations.

The supervisor is responsible for certain activities or results; he is presumably invested with the authority to achieve these. His set of authority and responsibility is interwoven with other sets to the end that all goals and functions of the organization are parceled out in small, manageable lots. This, of course, establishes a series of expectations: a single supervisor can perform his particular set of duties only upon the assumption that preceding or contiguous sets of duties have been, or are being carried out. At the same time, he is aware of the expectations of others that he will fulfill his functional role.

The structure of an organization establishes relationships between specified positions and specific expectations for these positions. The fact that these relationships and expectations are established is one thing; whether or not they are met is another.

PRESCRIPTIONS AND PROSCRIPTIONS

But let us return to the organizational influences which act to restrict the supervisor's exercise of leadership. These are the prescriptions and proscriptions generally in effect in all organizations, and those peculiar to a single organization. In brief these are the *thou shalt's* and the *thou shalt not's*.

Organizations not only prescribe certain duties for individual supervisory positions, they also prescribe specific methods and means of carrying out these duties and maintaining management-employee relations. These include rules, regulations, policy, and tradition. It does no good for the supervisor to say, *This seems to be the best way to handle such-and-such,* if the organization has established a routine for dealing with problems. For good or bad, there are rules that state that firings shall be executed in such a manner, accompanied by a certain notification; that training shall be conducted, and in this manner. Proscriptions are merely negative prescriptions; you may not discriminate against any employee because of politics or race; you shall not suspend any employee without following certain procedures and obtaining certain approvals.

Most of these prohibitions and rules apply to the area of interpersonal relations, precisely the area which is now arousing most interest on the part of administrators and managers. We have become concerned about the contrast between formally prescribed relationships and interpersonal relationships, and this brings us to the often discussed informal organization.

FORMAL AND INFORMAL ORGANIZATIONS

As we well know, the functions and activities of any organization are broken down into individual units of work called positions. Administrators must establish a pattern which will link these positions to each other and relate them to a system of authority and responsibility. Man-to-man are spelled out as plainly as possible for all to understand. Managers, then, build an official structure which we call the formal organization.

In these same organizations, employees react individually and in groups to institutionally determined roles. John, a worker, rides in the same carpool as Joe, a foreman. An unplanned communication develops. Harry, a machinist knows more about high-speed machining than his foreman or anyone else in his shop. An unofficial tool boss comes into being. Mary, who fought with Jane, is promoted over her. Jane now gives Mary's directions. A planned relationship fails to develop. The employees have built a structure which we call the informal organization.

Formal organization is a system of management-prescribed relations between positions in an organization.

Informal organization is a network of unofficial relations between people in an organization.

These definitions might lead us to the absurd conclusion that positions carry out formal activities and that employe4es spend their time in unofficial activities. We must recognize that organizational activities are in all cases carried out by people. The formal structure provides a needed framework within which interpersonal relations occur. What we call informal organization is the complex of normal, natural relations among employees. These personal relationships may be negative or positive. That is, they may impede or aid the achievement of organizational goals. For example, friendship between two supervisors greatly increases the probability of good cooperation and coordination between their sections. On the other hand, *buck passing* nullifies the formal structure by failure to meet a prescribed and expected responsibility.

It is improbable that an ideal organization exists where all activities are carried out in strict conformity to a formally prescribed pattern of functional roles. Informal organization arises because of the incompleteness and ambiguities in the network of formally prescribed relationships, or in response to the needs or inadequacies of supervisors or managers who hold prescribed functional roles in an organization. Many of these relationships are not prescribed by the organizational pattern; many cannot be prescribed; many should not be prescribed.

Management faces the problem of keeping the informal organization in harmony with the mission of the agency. One way to do this is to make sure that all employees have a clear understanding of and are sympathetic with that mission. The issuance of organizational charts, procedural manuals, and functional descriptions of the work to be done by divisions and sections helps communicate management's plans and goals. Issuances alone, of course, cannot do the whole job. They should be accompanied by oral discussion and explanation. Management must ensure that there is mutual understanding and acceptance of charts and procedures. More important is that management acquaint itself with the attitudes, activities, and peculiar brands of logic which govern the informal organization. Only through this type of knowledge can they and supervisors keep informal goals consistent with the agency mission.

SUPERVISION STATUS AND FUNCTIONAL ROLE

A well-established supervisor is respected by the employees who work with him. They defer to his wishes. It is clear that a superior-subordinate relationship has been established. That is, status of the supervisor has been established in relation to other employees of the same work group. This same supervisor gains the respect of employees when he behaves in as certain manner. He will be expected, generally, to follow the customs of the group in such matters as dress, recreation, and manner of speaking. The group has a set of expectations as to his behavior. His position is a functional role which carries with it a collection of rights and obligations.

The position of supervisor usually has a status distinct from the individual who occupies it: it is much like a position description which exists whether or not there is an incumbent. The status of a supervisory position is valued higher than that of an employee position both because of the functional role of leadership which is assigned to it and because of the status symbols of titles, rights, and privileges which go with it.

Social ranking, or status, is not simple because it involves both the position and the man. An individual may be ranked higher than others because of his education, social background, perceived leadership ability, or conformity to group customs and ideals. If such a man is ranked higher by the members of a work group than their supervisor, the supervisor's effectiveness may be seriously undermined.

If the organization does not build and reinforce a supervisor's status, his position can be undermined in a different way. This will happen when managers go around rather than through the supervisor or designate him as a straw boss, acting boss, or otherwise not a real boss.

Let us clarify this last point. A role, and corresponding status, establishes a set of expectations. Employees expect their supervisor to do certain things and to act in certain ways. They are prepared to respond to that expected behavior. When the supervisor's behavior does not conform to their expectations, they are surprised, confused, and ill-at-ease. It becomes necessary for them to resolve their confusion, if they can. They might do this by turning to one of their own members for leadership. If the confusion continues, or their attempted solutions are not satisfactory, they will probably become a poorly motivated, non-cohesive group which cannot function very well.

COMMUNICATION AND THE SUPERVISOR

In a recent survey, railroad workers reported that they rarely look to their supervisor for information about the company. This is startling, at least to us, because we ordinarily think of the supervisor as the link between management and worker. We expect the supervisor to be the prime source of information about the company. Actually, the railroad workers listed the supervisor next to last in the o5rder of their sources of information. Most surprising of all, the supervisors, themselves, stated that rumor and unofficial contacts were their principal sources of information. Here we see one of the reasons why supervisors may not be as effective as management desires.

The supervisor is not only being bypassed by his work group, he is being ignored, and his position weakened, by the very organization which is holding him responsible for the activities of his workers. If he is management's representative to the employee, then management has an obligation to keep him informed of its activities. This is necessary if he is to carry out his functions efficiently and maintain his leadership in the work group. The supervisor is expected to be a source of information; when he is not, his status is not clear, and employees are dissatisfied because he has not lived up to expectations.

By providing information to the supervisor to pass along to employees, we can strengthen his position as leader of the group, and increase satisfaction and cohesion within the group. Because he has more information than the other members, receives information sooner, and passes it along at the proper times, members turn to him as a source and also provide him with information in the hope of receiving some in return. From this, we can see an increase in group cohesiveness because:

- Employees are bound closer to their supervisor because he is *in the know*.
- There is less need to go outside the group for answers
- Employees will more quickly turn to the supervisor for enlightenment

The fact that he has the answers will also enhance the supervisor's standing in the eyes of his men. This increased status will serve to bolster his authority and control of the group and will probably result in improved morale and productivity.

The foregoing, of course, does not mean that all management information should be given out. There are obviously certain policy determinations and discussions which need not or cannot be transmitted to all supervisors. However, the supervisor must be kept as fully informed as possible so that he can answer questions when asked and can allay needless fears and anxieties. Further, the supervisor has the responsibility of encouraging employee questions and submissions of information. He must be able to present information to employees so that it is clearly understood and accepted. His attitude and manner should make it clear that he believes in what he is saying, that the information is necessary or desirable to the group, and that he is prepared to act on the basis of the information.

SUPERVISION AND JOB PERFORMANCE

The productivity of work groups is a product; employees' efforts are multiplied by the supervision they receive. Many investigators have analyzed this relationship and have discovered elements of supervision which differentiate high and low production groups. These researchers have identified certain types of supervisory practices which they classify as *employee-centered* and other types which they classify as *production centered*.

The difference between these two kinds of supervision lies not in specific practices but in the approach or orientation to supervision. The employee-centered supervisor directs most of his efforts toward increasing employee motivation. He is concerned more with realizing the potential energy of persons than with administrative and technological methods of increasing efficiency and productivity. He is the man who finds ways of causing employees to want to work harder with the same tools. These supervisors emphasize the personal relations between their employees and themselves.

Now, obviously, these pictures are overdrawn. No one supervisor has all the virtues of the ideal type of employee-centered supervisor. And, fortunately, no one supervisor has all the bad traits found in many production-centered supervisors. We should remember that the various practices that researchers have fond which distinguish these two kinds of supervision represent the many practices and methods of supervisors of all gradations between these extremes. We should be careful, too, of the implications of the labels attached to the two types. For instance, being production-centered is not necessarily bad, since the principal responsibility of any supervisor is maintaining the production level that is expected of his work group. Being employee-centered may not necessarily be good, if the only result is a happy, chuckling crew of loafers. To return to the researchers' findings, employee-centered supervisors:

- Recommend promotions, transfers, pay increases
- Inform men about what is happening in the company
- Keep men posted on how well they are doing
- Hear complaints and grievances sympathetically
- Speak up for subordinates

Production-centered supervisors, on the other hand, don't do those things. They check on employees more frequently, give more detailed and frequent instructions, don't give reasons for changes, and are more punitive when mistakes are made. Employee-centered supervisors were reported to contribute to high morale and high production, whereas production-centered supervision was associated with lower morale and less production.

More recent findings, however, show that the relationship between supervision and productivity is not this simple. Investigators now report that high production is more frequently associated with supervisory practices which combine employee-centered behavior with concern for production. (This concern is not the same, however, as anxiety about production, which is the hallmark of our production-centered supervisor.) Let us examine these apparently contradictory findings and the premises from which they are derived.

SUPERVISION AND MORALE

Why do supervisory activities cause high or low production? As the name implies, the activities of the employee-centered supervisor tend to relate him more closely and satisfactorily to his workers. The production-centered supervisor's practices tend to separate him from his group and to foster antagonism. An analysis of this difference may answer our question.

Earlier, we pointed out that the supervisor is a type of leader and that leadership is intimately related to the group in which it occurs We discover, now, that an employee-centered supervisor's primary activities are concerned with both his leadership and his group membership. Such a supervisor is a member of a group and occupies a leadership role in that group.

These facts are sometimes obscured when we speak of the supervisor as management's representative, or as the organizational link between management and the employee, or as the end of the chain of command. If we really want to understand what it is we expect of the supervisor, we must remember that he is the designated leader of a group of employees to whom he is bound by interaction and interdependence.

Most of his actions are aimed, consciously or unconsciously, at strengthening membership ties in the group. This includes both making members more conscious that he is a member of their group) and causing members to identify themselves more closely with the group. These ends are accomplished by:

- making the group more attractive to the worker: they find satisfaction of their needs for recognition, friendship, enjoyable work, etc.;
- maintaining open communication: employees can express their views and obtain information about the organization
- giving assistance: members can seek advice on personal problems as well as their work; and
- acting as a buffer between the group and management: he speaks up for his men and explains the reasons for management's decisions.

Such actions both strengthen group cohesiveness and solidarity and affirm the supervisor's leadership position in the group.

DEFINING MORALE

This brings us back to a point mentioned earlier. We had said that employee-centered supervisors contribute to high morale as well as to high production. But how can we explain units which have low morale and high productivity, or vice versa? Usually production and morale are considered separately, partly because they are measured against different criteria and partly because, in some instances, they seem to be independent of each other.

Some of this difficulty may stem from confusion over definitions of morale. Morale has been defined as, or measured by, absences from work, satisfaction with job or company, dissension among members of work groups, productivity, apathy or lack of interest, readiness to help others, and a general aura of happiness as rated by observers. Some of these criteria of morale are not subject to the influence of the supervisor, and some of them are not clearly related to productivity. Definitions like these invite findings of low morale coupled with high production.

Both productivity and morale can be influenced by environmental factors not under the control of group members or supervisors. Such things as plant layout, organizational structure and goals, lighting, ventilation, communications, and management planning may have an adverse or desirable effect.

We might resolve the dilemma by defining morale on the basis of our understanding of the supervisor as leader of a group; morale is the degree of satisfaction of group members with their leadership. In this light, the supervisor's employee-centered activities bear a clear relation to morale. His efforts to increase employee identification with the group and to strengthen his leadership lead to greater satisfaction with that leadership. By increasing group cohesiveness and by demonstrating that his influence and power can aid the group, he is able to enhance his leadership status and afford satisfaction to the group.

SUPERVISION, PRODUCTION, AND MORALE

There are factors within the organization itself which determine whether increased production is possible:

- Are production goals expressed in terms understandable to employees and are they realistic?
- Do supervisors responsible for production respect the agency mission and production goals?
- If employees do not know how to do the job well, does management provide a trainer—often the supervisor—who can teach efficient work methods?

There are other factors within the work group which determine whether increased production will be attained:

- Is leadership present which can bring about the desired level of production?
- Are production goals accepted by employees as reasonable and attainable?
- If group effort is involved, are members able to coordinate their efforts?

Research findings confirm the view that an employee-centered supervisor can achieve higher morale than a production-centered supervisor. Managers may well ask what is the relationship between this and production.

Supervision is production-oriented to the extent that it focuses attention on achieving organizational goals, and plans and devises methods for attaining them; it is employee-centered to the extent that it focuses attention on employee attitudes toward those goals, and plans and works toward maintenance of employee satisfaction.

High productivity and low morale result when a supervisor plans and organizes work efficiently but cannot achieve high membership satisfaction. Low production and high morale result when a supervisor, though keeping members satisfied with his leadership, either has not gained acceptance of organizational goals or does not have the technical competence to achieve them.

The relationship between supervision, morale, and productivity is an interdependent one, with the supervisor playing an integral role due to his ability to influence productivity and morale independently of each other.

A supervisor who can plan his work well has good technical knowledge, and who can install better production methods can raise production without necessarily increasing group satisfaction. On the other hand, a supervisor who can motivate his employees and keep them satisfied with his leadership can gain high production in spite of technical difficulties and environmental obstacles.

CLIMATE AND SUPERVISION

Climate, the intangible environment of an organization made up of attitudes, beliefs, and traditions, plays a large part in morale, productivity, and supervision. Usually when we speak of climate and its relationship to morale and productivity, we talk about the merits of *democratic* versus *authoritarian* climate. Employees seem to produce more and have higher morale in a democratic climate, whereas in an authoritarian climate, the reverse seems to be true or so the researchers tell us. We would do well to determine what these terms mean to supervision.

Perhaps most of our difficulty in understanding and applying these concepts comes from our emotional reactions to the words themselves. For example, authoritarian climate is usually painted as the very blackest kind of dictatorship. This is not surprising, because we are usually expected to believe that it is invariably bad. Conversely, democratic climate is drawn to make the driven snow look impure by comparison.

Now these descriptions are most probably true when we talk about our political processes, or town meetings, or freedom of speech. However, the same labels have been used by social scientists in other contexts and have also been applied to government and business organizations, without it, it seems, any recognition that the meanings and their social values may have changed somewhat

For example, these labels were used in experiments conducted in an informal classroom setting using 11-year-old boys as subjects. The descriptive labels applied to the climate of the setting as well as the type of leadership practiced. When these labels were transferred to a management setting, it seems that many presumed that they principally meant the king of leadership rather than climate. We can see that there is a great difference between the experimental and management settings and that leadership practices for one might be inappropriate for the other.

It is doubtful that formal work organizations can be anything but authoritarian, in that goals are set by management and a hierarchy exists through which decisions and orders from the top are transmitted downward. Organizations are authoritarian by structure and need; direction and control are placed in the hands of a few in order to gain fast and efficient decision making. Now this does not mean to describe a dictatorship. It is merely the recognition of the fact that direction of organizational affairs comes from above. It should be noted that leadership in some natural groups is, in this sense, authoritarian.

Granting that formal organizations have this kind of authoritarian leadership, can there be a democratic climate? Certainly there can be, but we would want to define and delimit this term. A more realistic meaning of democratic climate in organizations is the use of permissive and participatory methods in management-employee relations. That is, a mutual exchange of information and explanation with the granting of individual freedom within certain restricted and defined limits. However, it is not our purpose to debate the merits of authoritarianism versus democracy. We recognize that within the small work group there is a need for freedom from constraint and an increase in participation in order to achieve organizational goals within the framework of the organizational movement.

Another aspect of climate is best expressed by this familiar, and true, saying: actions speak louder than words. Of particular concern to us is this effect of management climate on the behavior of supervisors, particularly in employee-centered activities.

There have been reports of disappointment with efforts to make supervisors ore employee-centered. Managers state that, since research has shown ways of improving human relations, supervisors should begin to practice these methods. Usually a training course in human relations is established; and supervisors are given this training. Managers then sit back and wait for the expected improvements, only to find that there are none.

If we wish to produce changes in the supervisor's behavior, the climate must be made appropriate and rewarding to the changed behavior. This means that top-level attitudes and behavior cannot deny or contradict the change we are attempting to effect. Basic changes in organizational behavior cannot be made with any permanence, unless we provide an environment that is receptive to the changes and rewards those persons who do change.

IMPROVING SUPERVISION

Anyone who has read this far might expect to find *A Dozen Rules for Dealing With Employees* or *29 Steps to Supervisory Success*. We will not provide such a list.

Simple rules suffer from their simplicity. They ignore the complexities of human behavior. Reliance upon rules may cause supervisors to concentrate on superficial aspects of their relations with employees. It may preclude genuine understanding.

The supervisor who relies on a list of rules tends to think of people in mechanistic terms. In a certain situation, he uses *Rule No. 3*. Employees are not treated as thinking and feeling persons, but rather as figures in a formula: Rule 3 applied to employee X = Production.

Employees usually recognize mechanical manipulation and become dissatisfied and resentful. They lose faith in, and respect for, their supervisor, and this may be reflected in lower morale and productivity.

We do not mean that supervisors must become social science experts if they wish to improve. Reports of current research indicate that there are two major parts of their job which can be strengthened through self-improvement: (1) Work planning, including technical skills, and (2) motivation of employees.

The most effective supervisors combine excellence in the administrative and technical aspects of their work with friendly and considerate personal relations with their employees.

CRITICAL PERSONAL RELATIONS

Later in this chapter we shall talk about administrative aspects of supervision, but first let us comment on *friendly and considerate personal relations*. We have discussed this subject throughout the preceding chapters, but we want to review some of the critical supervisory influences on personal relations.

Closeness of Supervision: The closeness of supervision has an important effect on productivity and morale. Mann and Dent found that supervisors of low-producing units supervise very closely, while high-producing supervisors exercise only general supervision. It was found that the low-producing supervisors:

- check on employees more frequently
- give more detailed and frequent instructions
- limit employee's freedom to do job in own way

Workers who felt less closely supervised reported that they were better satisfied with their jobs and the company. We should note that the manner or attitude of the supervisor has an important bearing on whether employees perceive supervision as being close or general.

These findings are another way of saying that supervision does not mean standing over the employee and telling him what to do and when and how to do it. The more effective supervisor tells his employees what is required, giving general instructions.

COMMUNICATION

Supervisors of high-production units consider communication as one of the most important aspects of their job. Effective communication is used by these supervisors to achieve better interpersonal relations and improved employee motivation. Low-production supervisors do not rate communications as highly important.

High-producing supervisors find that an important aid to more effective communication is listening. They are ready to listen to both personal problems or interests and questions about the work. This does not mean that they are *nosey* or meddle in their employees' personal lives, but rather that they show a willingness to listen, and do listen, if their employees wish to discuss problems.

These supervisors inform employees about forthcoming changes in work; they discuss agency policy with employees; and they make sure that each employee knows how well he is doing. What these supervisors do is use two-way communication effectively. Unless the supervisor freely imparts information, he will not receive information in return.

Attitudes and perception are frequently affected by communication or the lack of it. Research surveys reveal that many supervisors are not aware of their employees' attitudes, nor do they know what personal reactions their supervision arouses. Through frank discussion with employees, they have been surprised to discover employee beliefs about which they were ignorant. Discussion sometimes reveals that the supervisor and his employees have totally different impressions about the same event. The supervisor should be constantly on the alert for misconceptions about his words and deeds. He must remember that, although his actions are perfectly clear to himself, they may be, and frequently are, viewed differently by employees.

Failure to communicate information results in misconceptions and false assumptions. What you say and how you say it will strongly affect your employees' attitudes and perceptions. By giving them available information, you can prevent misconceptions; by discussion, you may be able to change attitudes; by questioning, you can discover what the perceptions and assumptions really are. And it need hardly be added that actions should conform very closely to words.

If we were to attempt to reduce the above discussion on communication to rules, we would have a long list which would be based on one cardinal principle: Don't make assumptions!

- Don't assume that your employees know; tell them.
- Don't assume that you know how they feel; find out.
- Don't assume that they understand; clarify.

20 SUPERVISORY HINTS

1. Avoid inconsistency.
2. Always give employees a chance to explain their action before taking disciplinary action. Don't allow too much time for a "cooling off" period before disciplining an employee.
3. Be specific in your criticisms.
4. Delegate responsibility wisely.
5. Do not argue or lose your temper, and avoid being impatient.
6. Promote mutual respect and be fair, impartial, and open-minded.
7. Keep in mind that asking for employees' advice and input can be helpful in decision making.
8. If you make promises, keep them.
9. Always keep the feelings, abilities, dignity and motives of your staff in mind.
10. Remain loyal to your employees' interests.
11. Never criticize employees in front of others, or treat employees like children.
12. Admit mistakes. Don't place blame on your employees, or make excuses.
13. Be reasonable in your expectations, give complete instructions, and establish well-planned goals.
14. Be knowledgeable about office details and procedures, but avoid becoming bogged down in details.
15. Avoid supervising too closely or too loosely. Employees should also view you as an approachable supervisor.
16. Remember that employees' personal problems may affect job performance, but become involved only when appropriate.
17. Work to develop workers, and to instill a feeling of cooperation while working toward mutual goals.
18. Do not overpraise or underpraise, be properly appreciative.
19. Never ask an employee to discipline someone for you.
20. A complaint, even if unjustified, should be taken seriously.

NOTES

GENERAL PRINCIPLES OF WIRING

Section I. DESIGN AND LAYOUT OF INTERIOR WIRING

47. General

The different wiring systems in common use for civilian and armed forces construction are often called open-wire, cable, and conduit systems. Many installation methods and procedures used in the wiring processes are common to all systems, and these are described in this chapter. In most wiring installations the type of wiring to be installed will be specified on the blueprints. If not so specified the installation method must be determined. In general, the type of wiring used should be similar to that installed in adjacent or nearby buildings.

48. Load Per Outlet

The first step in planning the circuit for any wiring installation is the determination of the connected load per outlet. The load per outlet can be obtained in several different ways:

a. The most accurate method of determining load per outlet is made by obtaining the stated value from the blueprints or specifications.

   (1) Commonly, the lighting outlets shown on the blueprints are listed in the specifications along with their wattage rating.

      (*a*) If the lights used are of the incandescent type, this figure represents the total wattage of the lamp.

      (*b*) When fluorescent type lights are specified, the wattage drain (also called load per outlet) should be increased approximately 20 percent to provide for the ballast load. For example, when the fixture is rated as a 2-lamp, 100-watt unit, the actual wattage drain is 200 watts plus approximately 20 watts for each lamp ballast, or a total load of 240 watts.

   (2) If the specifications are not available, the blueprints in many cases designate the type of equipment to be connected to specific outlets. Though the equipment ultimately used in the outlet may come from a different manufacturer, equipment standards provide the electrician with assurance that the outlets will use approximately the same wattage. If the equipment is available, the nameplate will list the wattage used or ampere drain. If not, table VII should be used to obtain the average wattage consumption of electrical appliances. Table VIII lists the current requirements for small motors of various horsepower ratings.

b. To provide adequate wiring for systems where the blueprints or specifications do not list any special or appliance loads, the following general rules will apply:

   (1) For heavy duty outlets or mogul size lampholders, the load per outlet should be figured at 5 amperes each.

   (2) For all other outlets, both ceiling and wall, the wattage drain (load per outlet) should be computed at 1.5 amperes per outlet.

c. The total outlet load may also be determined on a watts-per-square-foot basis. In this load-determination method, the floor area of the building to be wired is computed from the outside dimensions of the building. This square footage area is then multiplied by the standard watts-per-square-foot requirement based on the type of building to be wired. Table IX lists these constants along with a feeder-demand factor which is explained in paragraph 53 for various types of building occupancies.

49. Type of Distribution

a. The electrical power load in any building cannot be properly circuited until the type and voltage of the central power-distribution system is known. The voltage and the number of wires from the

Table VII. Wattage Consumption of Electrical Appliances

Appliance	Average wattage
Blanket	150
Clock	3
Coffeemaker	550
Chafing dish	600
Dishwasher	100
Egg boiler	250
Fan, 8-inch	30
Fan, 10-inch	35
Fan, 12-inch	50
Frying pan	600
Griddle	450
Grill	600
Heater (radiant)	1000
Heating pad	50
Hotplate	660
Humidifier	500
Immersion heater	300
Iron	1000
Ironer	1320
Mixer	200
Phonograph	40
Range	8000
Refrigerator	250
Radio	100
Roaster	1320
Sewing machine	75
Soldering iron	200
Sunlamp	450
Television	300
Toaster	450
Vacuum cleaner	160
Washing machine	175
Water heater	2000
Waffle iron	660

Table VIII. Motor Currents

Horse-power	Full-load amperes			
	120 v. 1 phase	240 v. 1 phase	208 v. 3 phase	416 v. 3 phase
1/6	3.1	1.6	...	...
1/4	4.4	2.2	...	...
1/2	7.1	3.6	2.1	1.1
3/4	9.8	4.9	3.0	1.5
1	12.5	6.3	3.7	1.9
1 1/2	17.7	8.9	5.3	2.7
2	23.1	11.6	7.0	3.5
3	32.6	16.3	9.6	4.8
5	54.0	27.0	16.0	8.0

powerlines to the buildings are normally shown or specified on the blueprints. However, the electrician should check the voltage and type of distribution at the power-service entrance to every building in which wiring is to be done. This is especially necessary when he is altering or adding circuits. The voltage checks are usually made with an indicating voltmeter at the service-entrance switches or at the distribution load centers. The type of distribution is determined by visual check of the number of wires entering the building.

b. If only two wires enter the building, the service is either direct current or single-phase alternating current. The voltage is determined by an indicating voltmeter.

c. When three wires enter a building the service can either be single-phase, direct-current, or three-phase.

Table IX. Standard Loads for Branch Circuits and Feeders and Demand Factor for Feeders

Occupancy	Standard load, watts per square foot	Feeder demand factor, percent
Armories and auditoriums	1	100%
Banks	2	100%
Barber shops	3	100%
Churches	1	100%
Clubs	2	100%
Dwellings	3	100% for first 3,000 watts, 35% for next 117,000, 25% for excess above 120,000.
Garages	0.5	100%
Hospitals	2	40% for first 50,000 watts, 20% for excess over 50,000.
Office buildings	2	100% for first 20,000 watts, 70% for excess over 20,000.
Restaurants	2	100%
Schools	2	100% for first 15,000 watts, 50% for excess over 15,000.
Stores	3	100%
Warehouses	0.25	100% for first 12,500 watts, 50% for excess over 12,500.
Assembly halls	1	100%

(1) If the power distribution is single-phase alternating current or direct current the test leads over 2 of the wires in the service entrance will give an indicating voltmeter reading that will be exactly twice as much as when the voltmeter leads are applied between any 1 of these 2-wires and the third.

(2) A three-phase distribution system will show no change in voltage between any pair of leads when tested with an indicating voltmeter.

d. Four-wire distribution denotes 3-phase and neutral service. When tested, voltages between the neutral wires and each of the 3 hot wires should be all the same. The voltage readings between any 2 of these 3 wires are similar and should equal the neutral to hot wire voltage multiplied by 1.732. Common operating voltages for this type service are 120 and 208 volts.

50. Grounding

a. Requirements.
  (1) All electrical systems must have the neutral wire grounded if the voltage between the hot lead and the neutral is less than 150 volts.
  (2) It is recommended that all systems have a grounded neutral where the voltage to ground does not exceed 300 volts.
  (3) Circuits operating at less than 50 volts need not be grounded, provided the transformer supplying the circuit is connected to a grounded system.

b. Types of Grounding.
  (1) A system ground is the ground applied to a neutral wire. It reduces the possibility of fire and shock by reducing the voltage of 1 of the wires of a system to 0 volts potential above ground.
  (2) An equipment ground is an additional ground which is attached to appliances and machinery located in such places as laundries and basements where wet or humid conditions could create dangerous short circuits. An equipment ground is advantageous in these areas for the appliances can be maintained at zero voltage, and if a short circuit does occur in a hot load, the fuse protection opens the circuit and prevents serious injury to operating personnel.

c. Methods of Grounding.
  (1) A system ground is provided by the instal-

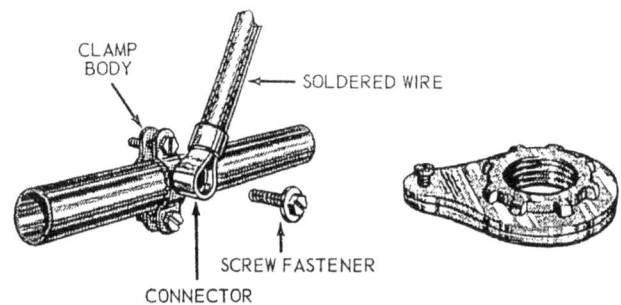

① CLAMP TYPE   ② BUSHING TYPE

Figure 42. Typical grounding fixtures.

lation of a No. 6-gage bare wire connecting the neutral wire either with a water pipe or a ¾-inch conduit driven 8 feet into the ground. The wire is attached to the water pipe or conduit by a special clamp or bushing ground-connector clamp after the pipe or conduit has been filed or sandpapered clean to make a good electrical contact. A clamp type ground-connector has two semicircular sections which encircle the ground rod or conduit and are tightened by a machine screw. A bushing type ground connector clamp is screwed onto the ground rod in a manner similar to installing a bushing on a conduit. Figure 42 shows typical grounding fixtures.

  (2) Equipment is grounded through the conduit in a permanent installation by utilizing the system ground, or through the use of a three-wire cord, plug, and matching receptacle. The third wire in the receptacle is attached to either the conduit or the system ground. Similarly, the third prong on the plug is connected to the metal structure of the equipment to be grounded.

d. Ground Detection. When testing or inspecting system installations, proper grounding can be determined visually and electrically as follows:
  (1) The neutral wire, always grounded, should be a white-colored insulated wire. The equipment ground wire should always be green.
  (2) If checked with an indicating voltmeter, the scale should indicate zero when the test prods are placed between the neutral wire and the building water pipes or ground rod.

51. Circuiting the Load

a. If all the power load in a building were con-

Table X. Requirements for Branch Circuits

Rating of circuit	15 amperes	20 amperes	25 amperes	35 amperes	50 amperes
Rubber-insulated conductors 2 or 3 per raceway or cable. Minimum gage number:					
(1) Type R	14	12	10	8	5
(2) Type RP	14	12	10	8	6
(3) Type RH	14	14	12	10	8
Receptacle rating (amperes)	15 (max.)	15 (min.)	20 (min.)	25 (min.)	50 (min.)
Type of lampholders (for exceptions, see National Electrical Code).	Any type.	Heavy duty.	Heavy duty.	Heavy duty.[1]	Heavy duty.[1]
Portable appliances. Maximum individual rating of one appliance, not motor-driven[2] (amperes).	12	15	20	Not permitted.	Not permitted.
Fixed appliances, total rating (amperes):					
(1) If lampholders or portable appliances are also supplied.	6	15	20	25	Combination not permitted.
(2) If fixed appliances only, with one or more being motor-driven, are supplied.	12	15	20	25	Not permitted.
(3) If fixed appliances only, none being motor-driven, are supplied.	15	20	25	35	50[3]

[1] No lampholder may be supplied by this circuit in dwellings.
[2] Can be motor-driven if time-lag fuses are used.
[3] Only appliances permitted on this circuit are fixed cooking appliances or a range and water heater.

nected to a single pair of wires and protected by a single fuse, the entire establishment would be without power in case of a breakdown, a short circuit, or a fuse blowout. In addition the wires would have to be large enough to handle the entire load, and, therefore, too large in some cases to make connections to individual devices. Consequently, the outlets in a building are divided into small groups known as branch circuits. These circuits normally are rated in amperes as shown in table X. This table contains a comparison of the various ampere requirements of the branch circuits with the standard circuit components.

b. The method of circuiting the building load varies with the size of the building and the power load.

(1) In a small building with little load, the circuit breakers or fuses are installed at the power-service entrance and the individual circuits are run from this location.

(2) For buildings of medium size with numerous wiring circuits, the fuse box should be located at the center of the building load so that all the branch runs are short, minimizing the voltage drop in the lines.

(3) When buildings are large or have the loads concentrated at several remote locations, the ideal circuiting would locate fuse boxes at each individual load center. It is assumed that the branch circuits would be radially installed at each of these centers to minimize the voltage drops in the runs.

c. The number of circuits required for adequate wiring can be determined by adding the connected load in watts and dividing the total by the wattage permitted on the size of branch circuit selected. The total wattage is obtained from the sum of the loads of each individual outlet determined by one of the three methods outlined in paragraph 48. For example, if 15-ampere, 110-volt circuits are to be used, the maximum wattage permitted on each circuit equals 15 x 110 or 1650 watts. If the total connected load is assumed to be 18,000 watts, $\frac{18000}{1650}$ shows 11.5 circuits are required. Since we cannot have ½ of a circuit, twelve 15-ampere circuits are used to carry the connected load. The number of circuits determined by this method is the basic minimum. For long-range planning in permanent installations, the best practice requires the addition of several circuits to the minimum required, or the installation of the next larger modular-size fusing panel to allow for future wiring additions. If additional circuits over the minimum required are used, reducing the number of outlets per circuit, the electrical installation is more efficient. This is true because the voltage drop in the system is reduced allowing the apparatus to operate more efficiently.

d. Motors which are used on portable appliances are normally disconnected from the power source either by removal of the appliance plug from its receptacle or by the operation of an attached built-in switch. Some large-horsepower motors, however, require a permanent power installation with special controls. Motor switches, some of which are shown in figure 43, are rated in horsepower capacity. In a single motor installation a separate circuit must be run from the fuse or circuit breaker panel to the motor, and individual fuses or circuit breakers installed. For multiple motor installations the National Electrical Code requires that "Two or more motors may be connected to the same branch circuit, protected at not more than 20 amperes at 125 volts or less or 15 amperes at 600 volts or less, if each does not exceed 1 horsepower in rating and each does not have a full load rating in excess of 6 amperes. Two or more motors of any rating, each with individual overcurrent protection (provided integral with the motor start switches or an individual units), may be connected to one branch circuit provided each motor controller and motor-running overcurrent device be approved for group installation and the branch circuit fusing rating be equal to the rating required for the largest motor plus an amount equal to the sum of the full load ratings of the other motors".

52. Balancing the Power Load on a Circuit

The ideal wiring system is planned so that each wiring circuit will have the same ampere drain at all times. Since this can never be achieved, the circuiting is planned to divide the connected load as evenly as possible. Thus, each individual circuit uses approximately the average power consumption for the total system. This will make for minimum service interruption. Figure 44 demonstrates the advantage of a balanced circuit when a 3-wire single-phase, 110–220-volt distribution system is used. The current in the neutral conductor remains 0 as shown.

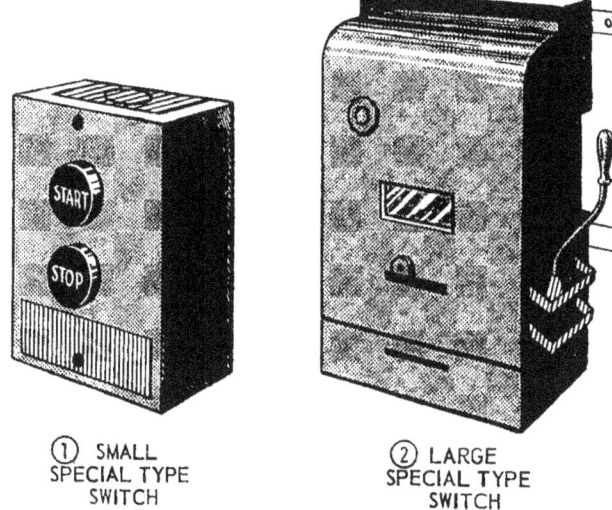

Figure 43. Motor switches.

This 1 factor reduces the voltage drop in each circuit by 50 percent from what it would be if the load were on two 2-wire circuits.

53. Load Per Building

a. Maximum Demand. In some building installations the total possible power load may be connected to power at the same time. In this case, the generating capacity of the power supply, which must be kept available for these buildings, is equal to the connected load. In the majority of building installations where armed forces personnel will work, the maximum load which the system is required to service is much less than the connected load. This power load which is set at some arbitrary figure below the possible total connected load is called the "maximum demand" of the building.

b. Demand Factor. The ratio of "maximum demand" to total connected load in a building expressed as a percentage is termed demand factor. The determination of building loads can be obtained by the use of standard demand factors as shown in table IX. For example, if the connected load in a warehouse is 22,500 watts, using the demand factors listed in table IX for warehouses the actual building load can be obtained as follows: 100 percent of the first 12,500 watts equals 12,500, 50 percent of the remaining 10,000 watts equals 5,000; therefore, the total building load is 12,500 plus 5,000 watts or 17,500 watts.

54. Balancing the Power Load of a Building

The standard voltage distribution system from a generating station to individual building installations is the 3- or 4-wire, 3-phase type. Distribution transformers as shown in figure 45 on the powerline poles change the voltage to 110 or 220, and are designed to deliver 3-wire single-phase service. These transformers are then connected across the distribution phase leads in a balanced arrangement as shown. Consequently, for maximum transformer efficiency, the building loads assumed for power distribution as shown in figure 45 should also be balanced as previously illustrated in figure 44.

55. Additions to Existing Wiring

a. Circuit Capacity. In the installation of additions to existing wiring in a building the electrician determines first the available extra capacity of the present circuits. This can readily be obtained by ascertaining the fused capacity of the building and subtracting the present connected load. If all the outlets do not have connected loads, their average load should be used to obtain the connected load figure. When the existing circuits have available capacity for new outlets and are located near the additional outlet required, they should be extended and connected to the new outlets.

b. New Circuits. When the existing outlets cannot handle an additional load and a spare circuit has been provided in the local fuse or circuit breaker panel, a new circuit is installed. This is also done if the new outlet or outlets are so located that a new circuit can be installed more economically than an existing circuit extension. Moreover, the installation of a new circuit will generally decrease the voltage drop on all circuits, resulting in an increase in appliance operating efficiency. Figure 46 illustrates the addition of a new circuit from the spare circuit No. 4 in the circuit breaker panel.

c. New Load Center. In many wiring installations no provisions are made for spare circuits in the fuse panel. Moreover, the location of the new circuit required is often remote from the existing fusing or circuit breaker panel. In this case the most favorable method of providing service to the circuit is to install a new load center at a location close to the circuit outlets. This installation must not overload the incoming service and service-entrance switch. Should such an overload be indicated, the service equipment should also be changed to suit the new requirements. This sometimes can be accomplished in 2-wire systems by pulling in an additional wire from the powerline. This changes the service from 2-wire to 3-wire at 110 to 220 volts. In these cases the fuse or circuit breaker box should also be changed and enlarged to accommodate the increased circuit capacity. Figure 47 schematically illustrates the installation of an additional load center for a new circuit.

d. Concealed Installations. The addition of outlets in a building with finished interior walls having enclosed air spaces entails the use of a fish wire and drop chain. Figure 48 shows the addition of a wire run for an outlet accomplished by a drop from the attic space or as a riser from the basement. First

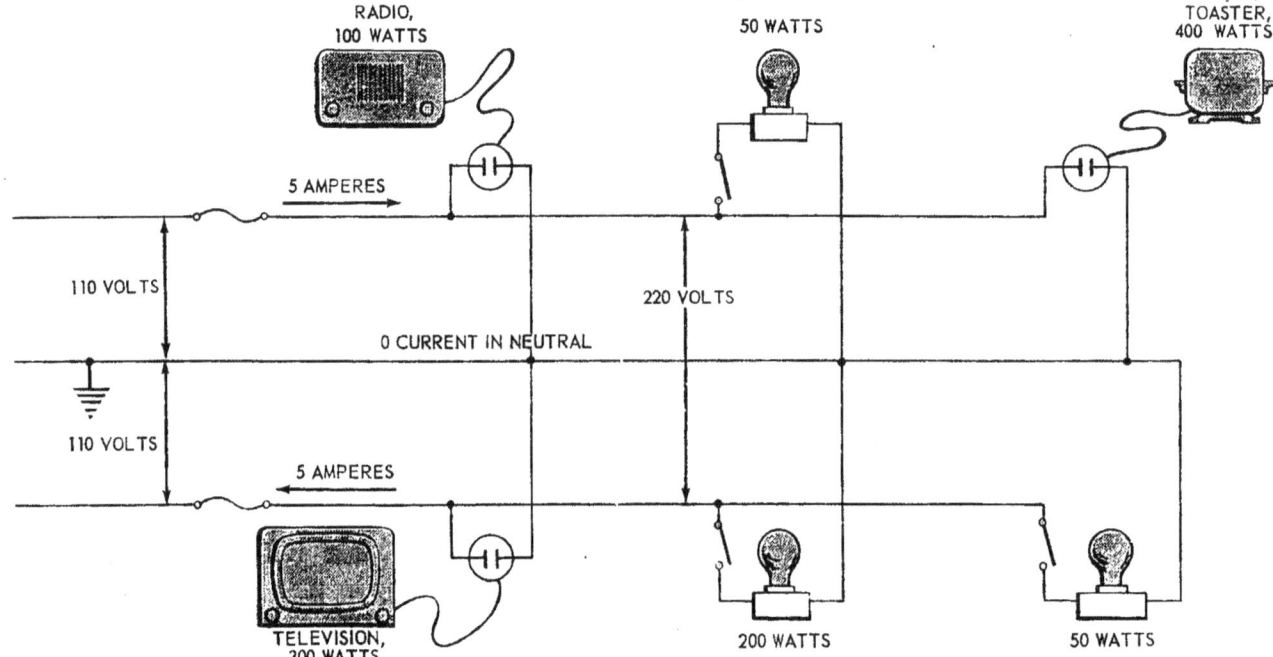

Figure 44. Diagram showing circuit balancing.

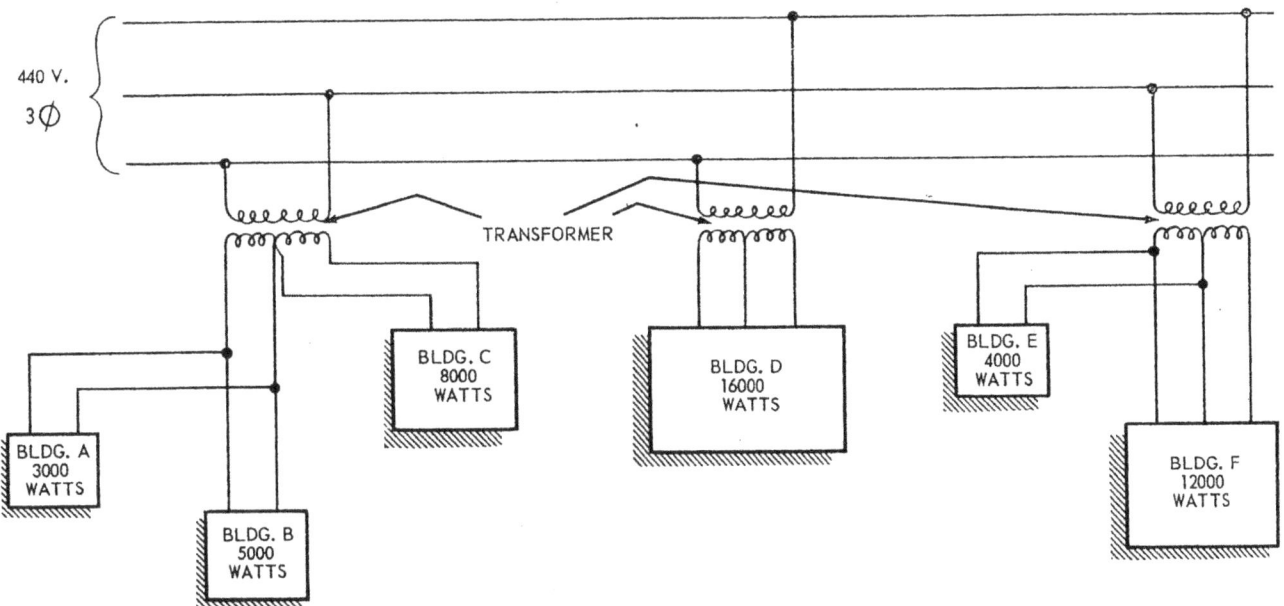

Figure 45. Diagram showing building load balancing.

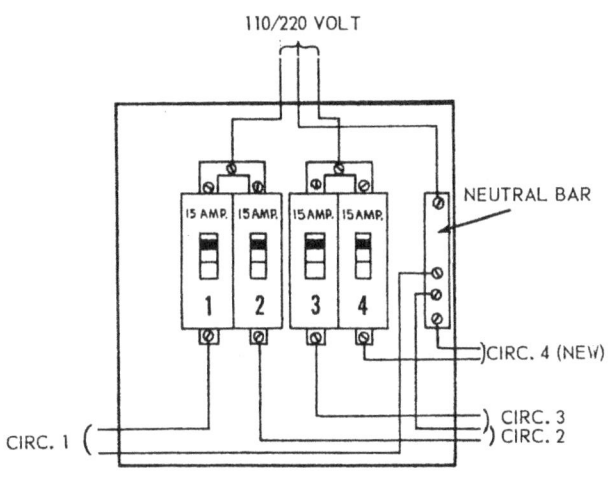

Figure 46. Addition of a new circuit.

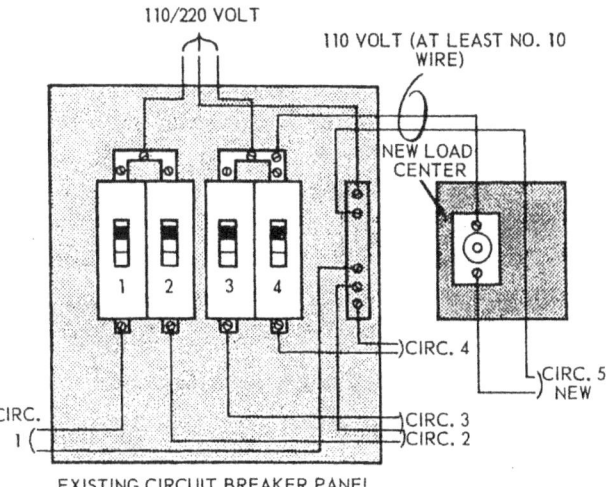

Figure 47. Addition of new load center.

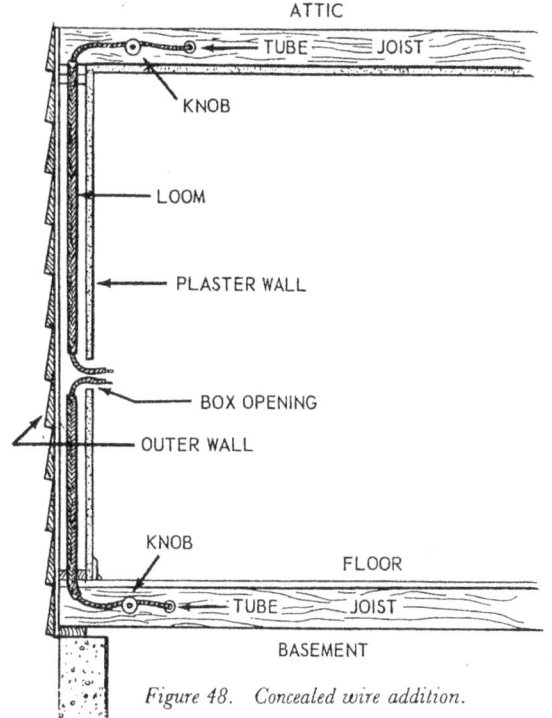

Figure 48. Concealed wire addition.

an opening is made in the interior finished wall at the desired outlet position. If the attic circuit is to be tapped, holes are drilled in the top plates of the wood studding, and a drop chain is lowered inside the wall and pulled through the box opening. The wire to be installed is then attached to the chain and pulled through, completing the rough-in operation for the outlet. Similarly when a wire is to be pulled in from the basement, a stiff wire, called a fish wire, is used. After drilling through the rough floor and bottom plate of the studding the fish wire is pushed up from the basement until it is grasped at the box opening. The wire to be pulled is then attached and pulled through the inner wall section.

56. Wire Size

a. Wire sizes No. 14 and larger are classified in accordance with their maximum allowable current-carrying capacity based on their physical behavior when subjected to the stress and temperatures of operating conditions. Fourteen-gage wire is the smallest wire size permitted for use in interior wiring systems.

b. The determination of the wire size to be used in circuits is dependent on the voltage drop coincident with each size. The size of the conductor used as a feeder to each circuit is also based on voltage drop, and should be selected so that the voltage drop from the branch circuit supply to the outlets will not be more than 3 percent for power loads and 1 percent for lighting loads. Table XI which is based on an allowable 3 percent voltage drop, lists the wire sizes required for various distances between supply and load, at the difference amperages.

c. Table XI also lists the service-wire requirements and capacities. The minimum gage for service-wire installation is No. 8 except for installations consisting of a single branch circuit in which case they shall not be smaller than the conductors of a branch circuit and in no case smaller than No. 12. Though this may seem to contradict the minimum wire size listed, the service-wire sizes are increased because they must not only meet the voltage-drop requirement but also be inherently strong enough to support their own weight, plus any additional loading caused by climatic conditions (ice, branches, and so on).

57. Special Switches

a. Three-Way Switching. A single-pole switch controls a light or a receptacle from only one location. When lights have to be controlled from more than one location, a 3-way switch is used. Three-way switches can be identified by a common terminal, normally color-coded darker than the other terminals and located alone at the end of the switch housing. A schematic wiring diagram of a 3-way switch with 3-wire cable is shown in figure 49. In the diagram terminals A and A' are the common terminals, and switch operation connects them either to B or C and B' and C' respectively. Either switch will operate to close or open the circuit, turning the lights on or off.

b. Four-Way Switching. Occasionally it is necessary to control an outlet or light from more than 2 locations. Two 3-way switches plus a 4-way switch for each location where control is desired and required in addition to that normally available in a 3-way circuit as illustrated in figure 50 (i. e., 3 control points, one 4-way switch, 4 control points, two 4-way switches). In figure 50 the switches must be installed with the 4-way units connected between the two 3-way units, and the 3-wire cable installed between the switches.

58. Wiring For Hazardous Locations

Hazardous locations requiring special wiring considerations are divided into four classes by the National Electric Code.

a. Class I. For locations in which highly flammable gasses and liquids are manufactured, used, or handled, such as hydrogen, gasoline, alcohol, etc., all wiring must be in rigid metal conduit with explosion-proof fittings. All equipment such as circuit breakers, fuses, motors, generators, controllers, etc., must be totally inclosed in explosion-proof housings.

b. Class II. In locations where combustible dust is likely to be thrown into suspension in the air in sufficient quantities to produce explosive mixtures, such as flour mills, grain elevators, coal pulverizing plants, etc., the wiring must be in rigid conduit with threaded fittings. All equipment must be in dust-proof cabinets with motors and generators totally inclosed or in totally inclosed fan-cooled housings.

c. Class III. Locations in which easily ignitible fibers or materials producing combustible flyings are handled or used, such as textile mills, cotton gins, or woodworking plants, require wiring of the same type as in Class II. If the atmosphere is such that lint and flyings will collect on motors or generators they must be inclosed as in Class II.

d. Class IV. In locations where easily combustible fibers are stored, such as warehouses for cotton waste, hemp, Spanish moss, excelsior, etc., all of the type of wiring described in this manual may be used. Open wiring is permitted when the conductors are protected where they are not run in roof spaces or well out of reach of mechanical damage. Rotating machines must be inclosed as in Class II.

59. Installation in Hazardous Locations

The Code further specifies standards for particular types of installations. For example, some of these special requirements for hospital operating room installation are listed in *a* through *f* below:

Table XI. Voltage Drop Tables

Wire size for 120-volt single-phase circuit

Load (amps.)	Minimum wire size (AWG)	Service wire size (AWG)	Wire size (AWG) — Distance one way from supply to load (ft.)												
			50	75	100	125	150	175	200	250	300	350	400	450	500
15	14	10	14	12	10	8	8	6	6	6	4	4	4	2	2
20	14	10	12	10	8	8	6	6	6	4	4	2	2	2	2
25	12	8	10	8	8	6	6	4	4	4	2	2	2	1	1
30	12	8	10	8	6	6	4	4	4	2	2	1	1	0	0
35	12	6	8	6	6	4	4	4	2	2	1	1	0	0	2/0
40	10	6	8	6	6	4	4	2	2	2	1	0	0	2/0	2/0
45	10	6	8	6	4	4	2	2	2	1	0	0	2/0	2/0	3/0
50	10	6	8	6	4	4	2	2	2	1	0	2/0	2/0	3/0	3/0
55	8	4	6	4	4	2	2	2	1	0	2/0	2/0	3/0	3/0	4/0
60	8	4	6	4	4	2	2	1	1	0	2/0	3/0	3/0	4/0	4/0
65	8	4	6	4	4	2	2	1	0	2/0	2/0	3/0	4/0	4/0	
70	8	4	6	4	2	2	1	1	0	2/0	2/0	3/0	4/0	4/0	
75	6	4	6	4	2	2	1	0	0	2/0	3/0	4/0	4/0		
80	6	4	6	4	2	2	1	0	0	2/0	3/0	4/0	4/0		
85	6	4	4	4	2	1	1	0	2/0	3/0	3/0	4/0			
90	6	2	4	2	2	1	0	0	2/0	3/0	4/0	4/0			
95	6	2	4	2	2	1	0	2/0	2/0	3/0	4/0				
100	4	2	4	2	2	1	0	2/0	2/0	3/0	4/0				

Wire size for 220-volt three-phase circuits

Load (amps.)	Minimum wire size (AWG)	Service wire size (AWG)	Wire size (AWG) — Distance one way from supply to load (ft.)												
			100	150	200	250	300	350	400	500	600	700	800	900	1,000
15	14	12	14	12	10	8	8	8	6	6	6	4	4	4	2
20	14	10	12	10	8	8	6	6	6	4	4	4	2	2	2
25	12	8	10	8	8	6	6	6	4	4	2	2	2	2	1
30	12	8	10	8	6	6	6	4	4	2	2	2	1	1	0
35	12	8	10	8	6	6	4	4	4	2	2	1	1	0	0
40	10	6	8	6	6	4	4	4	2	1	1	1	0	0	2/0
45	10	6	8	6	6	4	4	2	2	2	1	0	0	2/0	2/0
50	10	6	8	6	4	4	2	2	2	1	0	0	2/0	2/0	3/0
55	8	6	8	6	4	4	2	2	2	1	0	2/0	2/0	3/0	3/0
60	8	6	6	6	4	2	2	2	1	0	0	2/0	3/0	3/0	4/0
65	8	4	6	4	4	2	2	2	1	0	2/0	2/0	3/0	3/0	4/0
70	8	4	6	4	4	2	2	1	1	0	2/0	3/0	3/0	4/0	4/0
75	6	4	6	4	2	2	2	1	0	2/0	2/0	3/0	4/0	4/0	
80	6	4	6	4	2	2	1	1	0	2/0	3/0	3/0	4/0	4/0	
85	6	4	6	4	2	2	1	0	0	2/0	3/0	4/0	4/0		
90	6	4	6	4	2	2	1	0	0	2/0	3/0	4/0	4/0		
95	6	4	6	4	2	1	1	0	2/0	3/0	3/0	4/0			
100	4	2	4	2	2	1	0	0	2/0	3/0	4/0	4/0			
125	4	2	4	2	1	0	2/0	2/0	3/0	4/0					
150	2	2	2	2	0	2/0	2/0	3/0	4/0						
175	2	1	2	1	0	2/0	3/0	4/0	4/0						
200	1	0	1	0	2/0	3/0	4/0	4/0							
225	0	0	0	0	2/0	3/0	4/0								
250	2/0	2/0	2/0	2/0	3/0	4/0									
275	3/0	3/0	3/0	3/0	3/0	4/0									
300	3/0	3/0	3/0	3/0	4/0										
325	4/0	4/0	4/0	4/0											

Table is based upon approximately 3% voltage drop.

Table XI. Voltage Drop Tables—Continued

Wire size for 240-volt three-phase circuits.

Load (amps.)	Minimum wire size (AWG)	Service wire size (AWG)	Wire size (AWG) Distance one way from supply to load (ft.)												
			100	150	200	250	300	350	400	500	600	700	800	900	1,000
15	14	10	14	12	10	9	8	6	6	6	4	4	4	2	2
20	14	10	12	10	8	8	6	6	6	4	4	2	2	2	2
25	12	8	10	8	8	6	6	4	4	4	2	2	2	1	1
30	12	8	10	8	6	6	4	4	4	2	2	1	1	0	0
35	12	6	8	6	6	4	4	4	2	2	1	1	0	0	2/0
40	10	6	8	6	6	4	4	2	2	2	1	0	0	2/0	2/0
45	10	6	8	6	4	4	2	2	2	1	0	0	2/0	2/0	3/0
50	10	6	8	6	4	4	2	2	2	1	0	2/0	2/0	3/0	3/0
55	8	4	6	4	4	2	2	2	1	0	2/0	2/0	3/0	3/0	4/0
60	8	4	6	4	4	2	2	1	1	0	2/0	3/0	3/0	4/0	4/0
65	8	4	6	4	4	2	2	1	0	2/0	2/0	3/0	4/0	4/0	
70	8	4	6	4	2	2	1	1	0	0	2/0	3/0	4/0	4/0	
75	6	4	6	4	2	2	1	0	0	2/0	3/0	4/0	4/0		
80	6	4	6	4	2	2	1	0	0	2/0	3/0	4/0	4/0		
85	6	4	4	4	2	1	1	0	2/0	3/0	3/0	4/0			
90	6	2	4	2	2	1	0	0	2/0	3/0	4/0	4/0			
95	6	2	4	2	2	1	0	2/0	2/0	3/0	4/0				
100	4	2	4	2	2	1	0	2/0	2/0	3/0	4/0				
125	4	2	4	2	1	0	2/0	3/0	3/0	4/0					
150	2	1	2	1	0	2/0	3/0	4/0	4/0						
175	2	0	2	0	2/0	3/0	4/0	4/0							
200	1	0	1	0	2/0	3/0	4/0								
225	1/0	2/0	1/0	2/0	3/0	4/0									
250	2/0	2/0	2/0	2/0	3/0	4/0									
275	3/0	3/0	3/0	3/0	4/0										
300	3/0	3/0	3/0	3/0	4/0										
325	4/0	4/0	4/0	4/0											

Table is based on approximately 3% voltage drop.

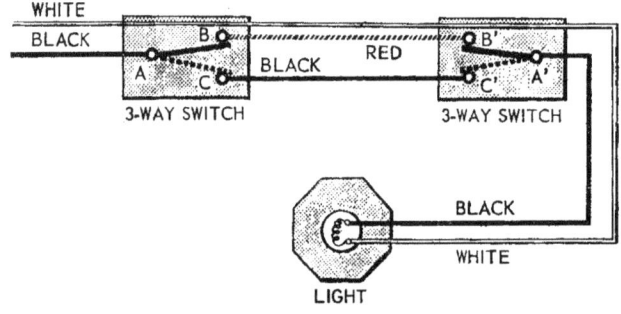

Figure 49. Three-way switch wiring.

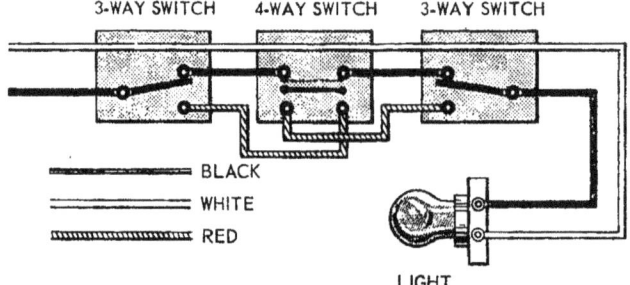

Figure 50. Four-way switch wiring.

a. All equipment installed in the operating room must be explosion proof and provided with a suitable equipment ground.

b. In anaesthetizing locations, an ungrounded electrical distribution system is required to reduce the hazards of electric shocks and arcs in the event of insulation failure. Alternating-current circuits shall be insulated from the conventionally grounded alternating supply by means of one or more transformers which isolate the circuits electrically from the main feeder line. Direct-current circuits shall be insulated from their grounded feeders by means of a motor generator set or suitable battery system.

c. All service equipment including switch and panel boards must be installed in nonhazardous locations.

d. Ceiling suspended lighting fixtures shall be suitably protected against mechanical injury.

e. Explosion-proof switches, receptacles, motors or similar conduit installations must be isolated from the rest of the conduit runs by sealing fittings. This type fitting has a removable plug which permits the insertion of a sealing compound, sealing off the points of possible explosion from the remaining conduit areas.

f. Nonmetallic tools such as rubber head hammers and spark free drills must always be used when making electrical repairs or installations in the area.

Section II. BASIC PROCEDURES COMMON TO ALL WIRING

60. Splices

A spliced wire must be as good a conductor as a continuous conductor. Figure 51 shows many of the variations of splicing used to obtain an electrically-secure joint. Though splices are permitted wherever accessible in wiring systems they should be avoided whenever possible. The best wiring practice (including open wiring systems) is to run continuous wires from the service box to the outlets. Under no conditions should splices be made in conductors encased in conduit.

61. Solderless Connectors

Figure 52 illustrates several types of connectors used in place of splices because of their ease of installation. Since heavy wires are difficult to tape and solder properly, split-bolt connectors (fig. 52 ①) are commonly used for wire joining. Figure 52 ②

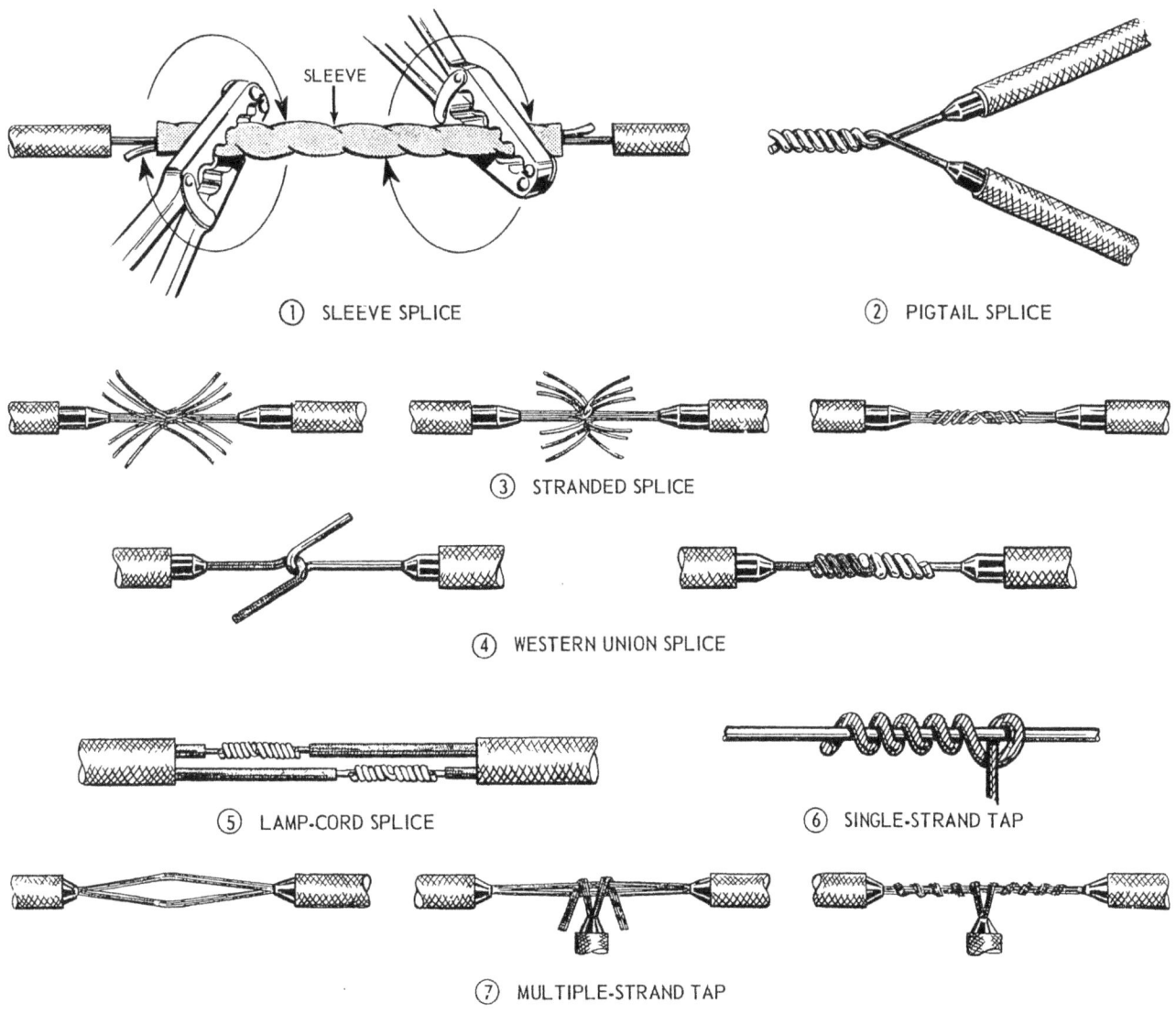

Figure 51. Typical wire splices and taps.

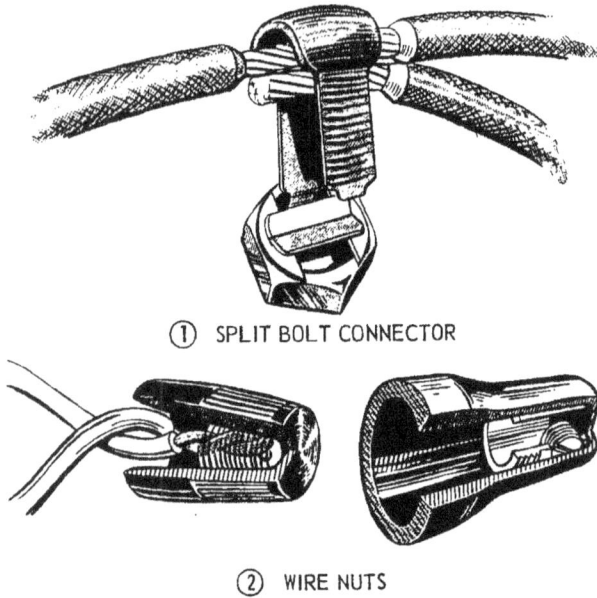

① SPLIT BOLT CONNECTOR

② WIRE NUTS

Figure 52. Solderless connectors.

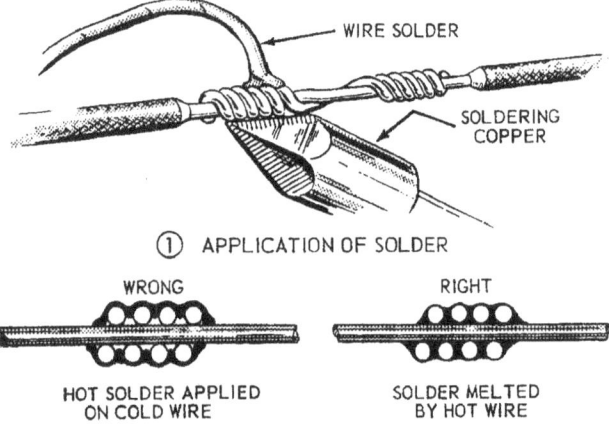

① APPLICATION OF SOLDER

② RIGHT AND WRONG SOLDER JOINT

Figure 53. Soldering and solder joints.

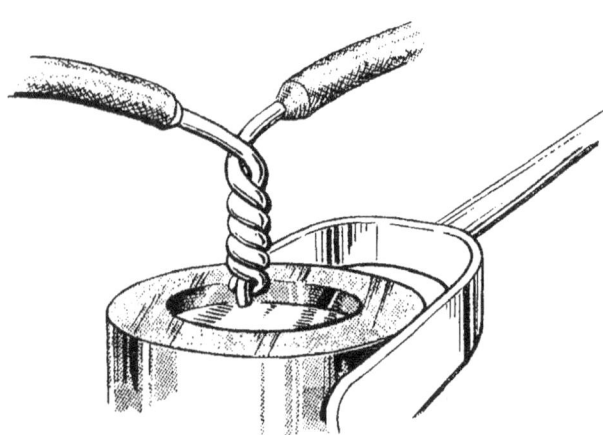

Figure 54. Dip soldering.

illustrates several types of solderless connectors popularly called wire nuts, which are used for connecting small-gage and fixture wire. One design shown consists of a funnel-shaped metal-spring insert molded into a plastic shell, into which the wires to be joined are screwed. The other type shown has a removable insert which contains a setscrew to clamp the wires. The plastic shell is screwed onto the insert to cover the joint.

62. Soldering

a. All splices must be soldered before they are considered to be as good as the original conductor. The primary requirements for obtaining a good solder joint are a clean soldering iron, a clean joint, and a nonacid flux. These requirements can be satisfied by using pure rosin on the joint, or by using a rosin-core solder.

b. To insure a good solder joint, the electric heated or copper soldering iron should be applied to the joint until the joint melts the solder by its own heat. Figure 53 ② shows the difference between a good and bad solder joint. The bad joint has a weak crystalline structure.

c. Figure 54 illustrates dip soldering. This method of soldering is frequently used by experienced electricians because of its convenience and relative speed for soldering pigtail splices. These splices are the most common type used in interior wiring.

63. Taping Joints

a. Every soldered joint must be covered with a coating of rubber, or varnished cambric, and friction tape to replace the wire insulation of the conductor. In taping a spliced solder joint (fig. 55) the rubber or cambric tape is started on the tapered end of the wire insulation and advanced toward the other end, with each succeeding wrap, by overlap-

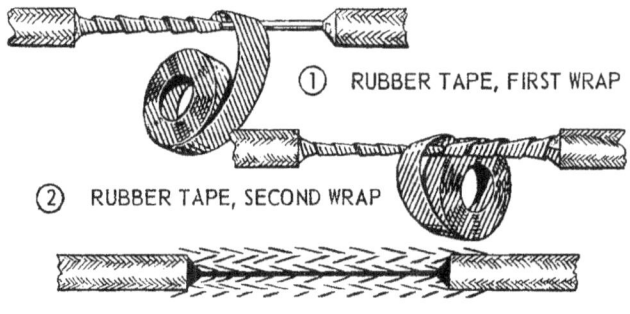

① RUBBER TAPE, FIRST WRAP

② RUBBER TAPE, SECOND WRAP

③ RUBBER AND FRICTION TAPED JOINT

Figure 55. Rubber- and friction-tape insulating.

ping the windings. This procedure is repeated from one end of the splice to the other until the original insulation thickness has been restored. The joint is then covered with several layers of friction tape.

b. Though the method in *a* above for taping joints is still considered to be standard, the scotch electrical tape, which serves as an insulation and a protective covering, should be used whenever available. This tape materially reduces the time required to tape a joint, and reduces the space needed by the joint because a satisfactory protective and insulation covering can be achieved with single-layer taping.

64. Insulation and Making Wire Connections

a. When attaching a wire to a switch or an electrical device or when splicing it to another wire, the wire insulation must be removed to bare the copper conductor. Figure 56 ① shows the right and wrong way to remove insulation. When the wire-stripping tool is applied at right angles to the wire, there is danger that the wire may be nicked and thus weakened. This may result in a short circuit. Consequently the cut is made at an angle to the conductor. After the protective insulation is removed, the conductor is scraped or sanded thoroughly to remove all traces of insulation and oxide on the wire.

b. Figures 56 ② and ③ show the correct method of attaching the trimmed wire to terminals. The wire loop is always inserted under the terminal screw, as shown, so that the tightening process tends to close the loop. The loop is made so that the wire insulation terminates close to the terminal.

65. Job Sequence

a. General. The installation of interior wiring is generally divided into two major divisions called roughing-in and finishing. Roughing-in is the installation of the outlet boxes, cable, wire, and conduit. Finishing is the installation of the switches, receptacles, covers, fixtures, and the completion of the service. The interval between these two work periods is used by other trades for plastering, inclosing walls, finishing floors, and trimming.

b. Roughing-In.

(1) The first step in the roughing-in phase of a wiring job is the mounting of outlet boxes. The mounting can be expedited if the locations of all boxes are first marked on the studs and joists of the building.

(2) All of the boxes are mounted on the building members on their own or by special brackets. For concealed installation, all boxes must be installed with the forward edge or plaster ring of the boxes flush with the finished walls. Figure 25 illustrates typical box mountings.

(3) The circuiting and installation of wire for open wiring, cable, or conduit should be the next step. This involves the drilling and cutting-out of the building members to allow for the passage of the conductor or its protective covering. The production-line method of drilling the holes for all runs, as the installations between boxes are called, at one time, and then installing all of the wire, cable, or conduit, will expedite the job.

(4) The final roughing-in step in the installation of conduit systems is the pulling-in of wires between boxes. This can also be included as the first step in the finishing phase, and requires care in the handling of the wires to prevent the marring of finished wall or floor surfaces.

c. Finishing.

(1) The splicing, soldering, and taping of joints in the outlet boxes is the intial step in the completion phase of a wiring job.

(2) Upon completion of the first finishing step, the proper leads to the terminals of

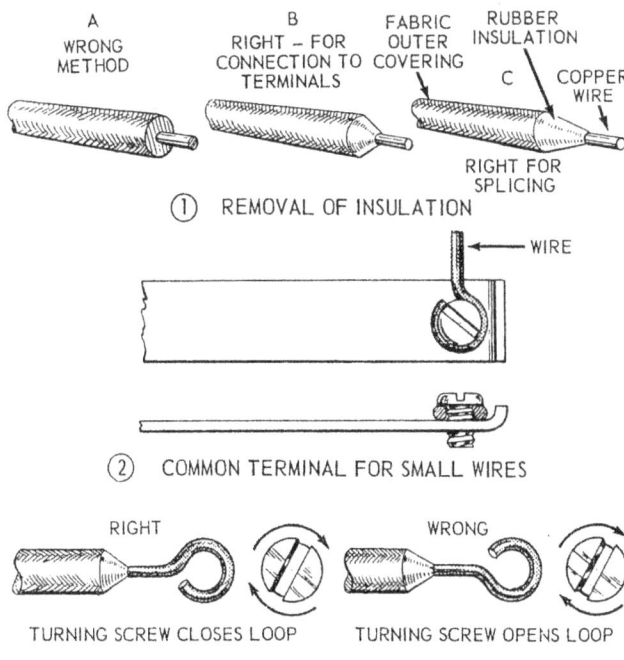

Figure 56. Removing insulation and attaching wire to terminals.

switches, ceiling and wall outlets, and fixtures are then installed.

(3) The devices and their cover plates are then attached to the boxes. The fixtures are generally supported by the use of special mounting brackets called fixture studs or hickeys.

(4) The service-entrance cable and fusing or circuit breaker panels are then connected and the circuits fused.

(5) The final step in the wiring of any building requires the testing of all outlets by the insertion of a test prod or test lamp, the operation of all switches in the building, and the loading of all circuits to insure proper circuiting has been installed.

OPEN WIRING, KNOBS, AND TUBES

Section I. INSTALLATION

66. Advantages and Uses

Open wiring is permitted by the National Electrical Code for interior use. A cost comparison of the four basic types of wiring indicates open wiring to be the most economical. This is true only because the costs of the materials used in installation are comparatively low when compared to the other systems. If the labor costs were computed, this system may be equal or higher in cost than the other methods of installation, especially when a great amount of damage-protection installation is needed. Installations of open wiring, however, are very common during wartime periods of material shortages.

67. Materials

a. Conductors. Conductors for open wiring in dry places may be any one of the rubber-covered (R, RP, RH, or RHT), slow-burning, weatherproof (SBW), varnish-cambric (V), or thermoplastic (T or TW) types. In damp locations, conductors should always be of the rubber-covered type.

b. Insulators. Insulators should be free of projections or sharp edges that might cut into and injure the insulation. They are commonly made of porcelain. Loom, which is a flexible nonmetallic tubing, is also used to protect the electrical conductors.

c. Boxes and Devices. Boxes and devices used with open wiring are described in paragraph 31.

68. Wire Spacing

In an exposed installation of knob-and-tube wiring, the wires must be separated from each other by at least 2½ inches. They must be spaced at least ½ inch from the building surface in a dry location, and at least 1 inch when in a wet or damp location. In a concealed installation the wires must be separated a distance of at least 3 inches and must be supported at least 1 inch from the mounting surface. The minimum spacing of wires in straight runs and at right angle turns is illustrated in figures 57 and 58.

69. Support Spacing

a. Run Spacing. When wiring is run over exposed flat surfaces, the knobs and cleats should be spaced no further than 4½ feet apart as shown in figure 59.

b. Tap Spacing. A support should be installed within 6 inches of a wire tap or takeoff. The wire of the tap circuit should always be secured to this support to insure a strain-free tap.

c. Support Spacing from Boxes. Supports should be installed within 12 inches of an outlet box. The wires to the box should be installed loosely so that there is no strain on the terminal connections.

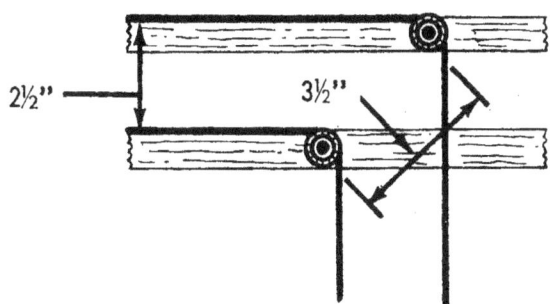

Figure 57. Wire spacing for exposed work.

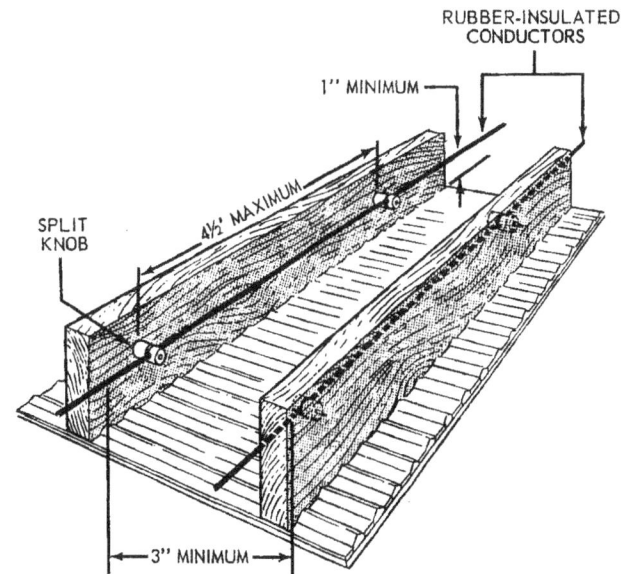

Figure 58. Minimum wire spacing for concealed installation.

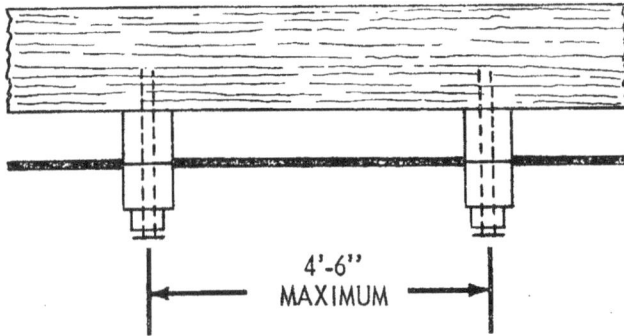

Figure 59. Knob and cleat spacing.

70. Installation

a. Typical Installation. Figure 60 shows a typical exposed knob-and-tube installation for a hospital unit, and demonstrates the circuiting and the methods of installing the conductors to each of the outlets.

b. Knobs and Cleats.

(1) Split knobs are used to support wire sizes 10 through 14 and can support 1 or 2 wires. They are used as 2-wire supports at splices and taps. Figure 61 ① illustrates the use of split knobs.

(2) Solid knobs are employed to support wire size No. 8 or larger. The wires must be supported on the solid knobs by tying. The conductors used for tying must have the same insulation as the supported conductors. A porcelain solid knob is shown in figure 61 ②.

(3) Two- or three-wire cleats are also used in supporting wire sizes No. 10 to 14. Single cleats must be used for wire size No. 8 or larger. Cleats are available which support the wires at distances of ½ to 1 inch from the surface on which the cleats are mounted.

(4) The installation steps used in mounting the split knobs or cleats for supporting wires are shown in figure 61. In the first operation, leather washers, to cushion the porcelain, are threaded on the nails of a 2-wire cleat. In the second step 2 wires are placed in the grooves of the cleat base section and the cleat head and nails are positioned above the wires. The third step shows the cleat in supporting position after the wires have been pulled tight and the nails driven firmly into the wood.

c. Wire Protectors.

(1) *Tubes.* When conductors pass through

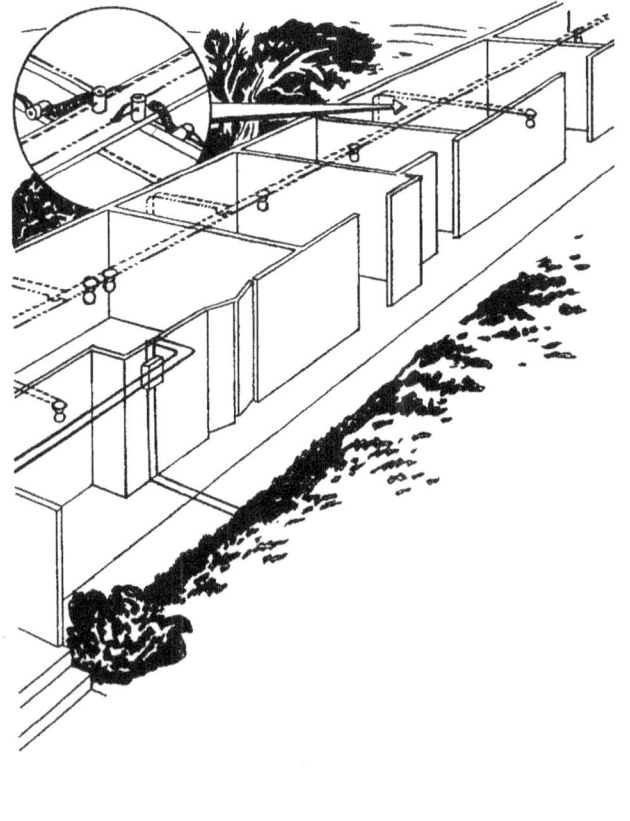

Figure 60. Typical knob-and-tube installation

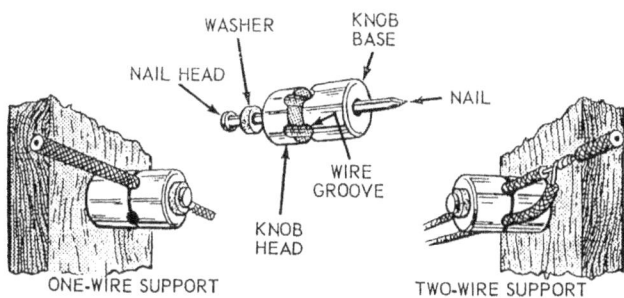

① PORCELAIN SPLIT KNOB SUPPORTING ONE OR TWO WIRES

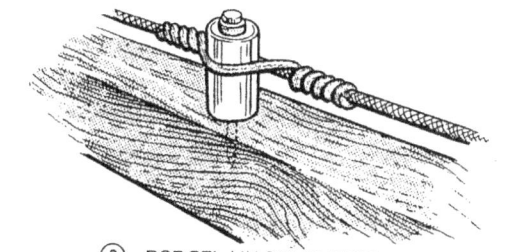

② PORCELAIN SOLID KNOB

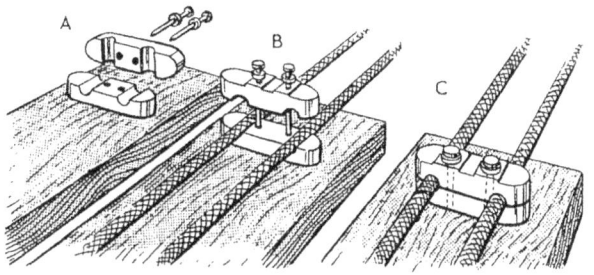

③ PORCELAIN CLEATS SUPPORTING TWO PARALLEL WIRES

Figure 61. Knob and cleat installation.

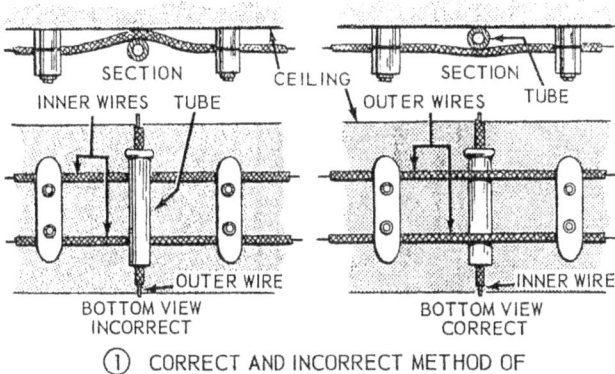

① CORRECT AND INCORRECT METHOD OF INSTALLING PROTECTIVE TUBE FOR WIRE CROSSOVER

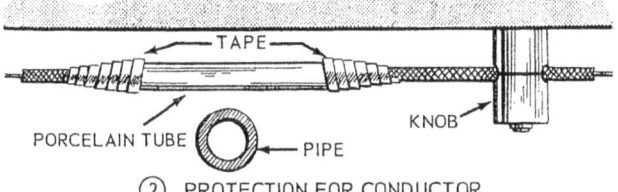

② PROTECTION FOR CONDUCTOR PASSING OVER PIPE

Figure 62. Protective tubes for conductors.

studs, joists, floors, walls, or partitions they must be protected by porcelain tubes installed in the hole through the supporting members. These tubes are available in standard sizes ranging from 1 to 24 inches long and 6/16 to 1½ inch inner diameter. The tubes must be long enough to extend through the entire wall. If the wall is too thick to use porcelain bushings, standard iron pipe or conduit may be used, provided insulated bushings are installed at each end of the pipe. The holes in which the tubes are to be installed should be drilled at an angle so that the tube head can be placed on the high side of the hole to prevent it from being dislodged by gravity. The tubes may also be used to protect wires at points of crossover. As the tube is installed on the wire closest to the supporting surface, it is always installed on the inner wire, thus preventing the outer wires from making contact with the mounting surface.

Figure 62 illustrates the proper and improper use of tubes at points of wire crossover and also the use of a tube installation for protecting an electrical conductor passing over a pipe. Conductors passing through timber cross braces in plastered partitions must be protected by an additional tube extending at least 3 inches above the timber. The extra tubes (fig. 63) protect the conductors from plaster accumulation, which collects on the horizontal cross members when plastering.

(2) *Loom.* In some installations where it is difficult to support wires on knobs and cleats, the wires may be encased in a continuous flexible tubing, commonly called loom. This tubing which is fabricated of woven varnished cambric, should be supported on the building by means of knobs, spaced approximately 18 inches apart. Any such run should not exceed a distance of 15 feet. Loom is also used to insulate wires at crossovers when they are installed closer than ½ inch to supporting timbers, when 2 or more wires are spaced less than 2½ inches apart, or upon entry to an outlet box. Outlet boxes used in open wiring are designed for the secure clamping of the loom wire to the box. Figure 64 illustrates typical uses of loom.

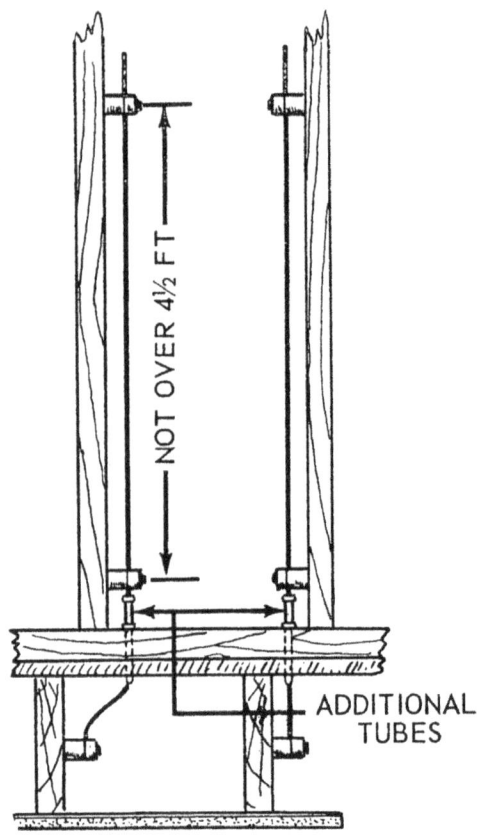

Figure 63. Additional tubes to protect against plaster accumulation.

d. *Damage Protection.*

(1) *Running boards.* When conductors are installed where they may be subject to mechanical damage, protective shields called running boards must be used. Exposed open wiring located within 7 feet of the floor is considered to be subject to mechanical injury. The required installations of a running board on the rafters and below joists for preventing such injury is pictured in figure 65 1 . Running boards must be at least ½ inch thick and must extend at least 1 inch but not more than 2 inches outside of the conductors. This method of installation is used when the wires are threaded through the joists and rafters. In some installations the wires have to be installed on the running boards with protective sides called railings.

(2) *Railings.* Railings should be at least ⅞ inch thick and when used alone are at least as high as the insulating supports. When used with running boards they are at least 2 inches high. Figure 65 2 illustrates the installation of railings with and without a running board.

(3) *Boxing.* The preferred method of protecting open wiring on walls within 7 feet of the floor is called boxing. This method requires the installation of railings with a cover spaced at least 1 inch from the conductor. In this installation, the boxing should be closed at the top and bushings installed to protect the entering and leaving wire leads.

(4) *Protection limitations.* As previously outlined and illustrated the labor and expense of installing damage protection in open wiring is extensive. Consequently, open wiring installations should be limited to wiring layouts whose outlet locations do not require damage protection. Nonconforming installations may be made in emergencies where the possibility of mechanical damage is not present.

e. *Three-Wire Installations.* The installation of wires in groups of 3 on joists and running boards requires that those surfaces be at least 7 inches wide to insure wire spacing of 2½ inches and a space of 1 inch for wood clearance beyond each outside wire. When joists are not large enough, 1 wire may be run on

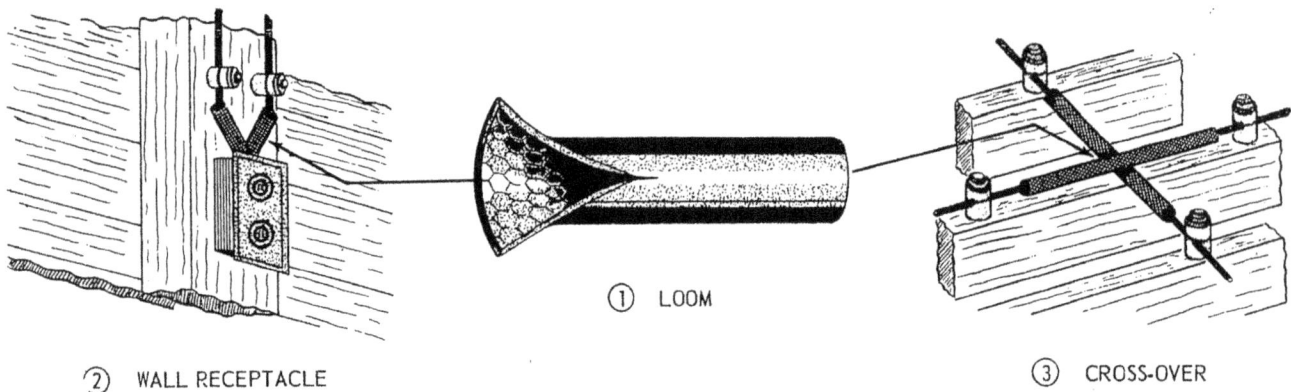

Figure 64. Typical insulation of wires with loom.

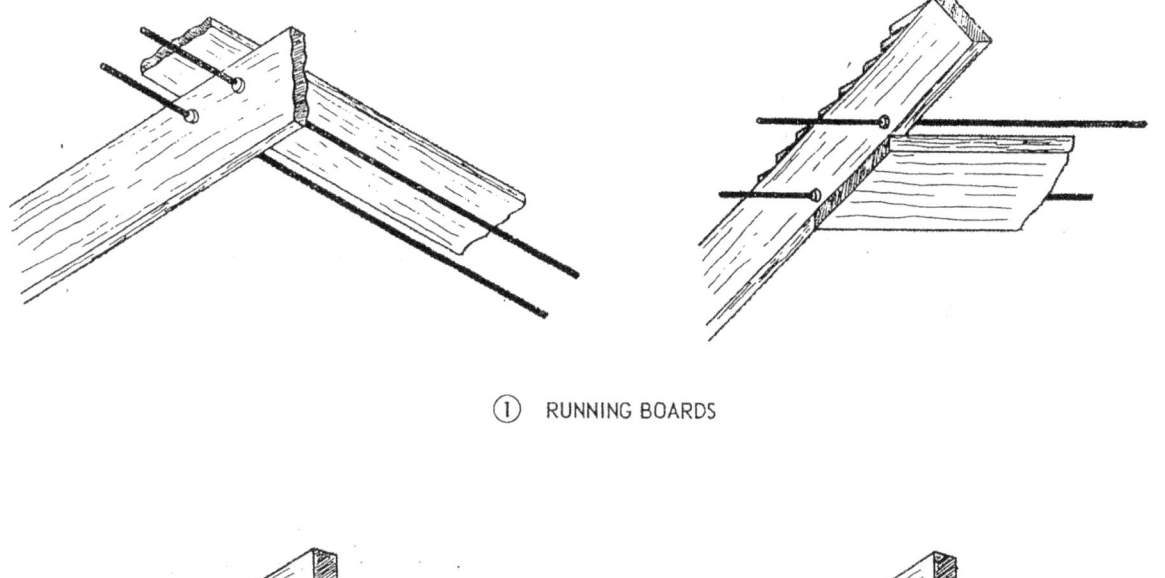

① RUNNING BOARDS

② RAILINGS

Figure 65. Protection for wiring subject to damage.

the top of the joist and the other 2 wires on the sides. Typical installations of 3 wires on joists and running boards are shown in figure 66.

f. Concealed Installation. Concealed knob-and-tube wiring consists of conductors supported in the hollow spaces of walls and ceilings. The wiring is installed in buildings under construction after the floors and studdings are in place, but before lathing or any other construction is completed. The wires are attached to devices in boxes which must have their front edges mounted flush with the finished surface. To facilitate this type of installation, the boxes are generally mounted on brackets or wooden cleats as shown in figure 67.

71. Connection to Devices

a. Figure 68 shows the procedure used in connecting electrical lighting devices to an open wiring circuit. The base of the porcelain lamp socket is first fastened by wood screws to the mounting member. The wires are then stripped of insulation and looped around the screw terminals. Finally, the porcelain head is attached to the base.

b. A typical duplex receptacle installation for an open wiring installation (fig. 69) illustrates the required knob mounting 12 inches from the box, and the placement of loom over the wire at the box entry. The standard mounting height of a receptacle is either 1 foot or 4 feet above the floor depending upon the location of the outlet.

c. The installation and connection of lampholders commonly used in exposed open wiring is shown in figure 70. The pigtail socket has permanently attached leads of No. 14 wire size or larger. These are paired, but are not twisted together unless they are longer than 3 feet. The pendant lampholder is a device to which the lamp cord is attached and supported by means of an underwriters knot. Both the pendant and pigtail lampholder sockets are keyless (no switch) and are operated by wall switches to prevent additional strain on the lead wires supporting the sockets.

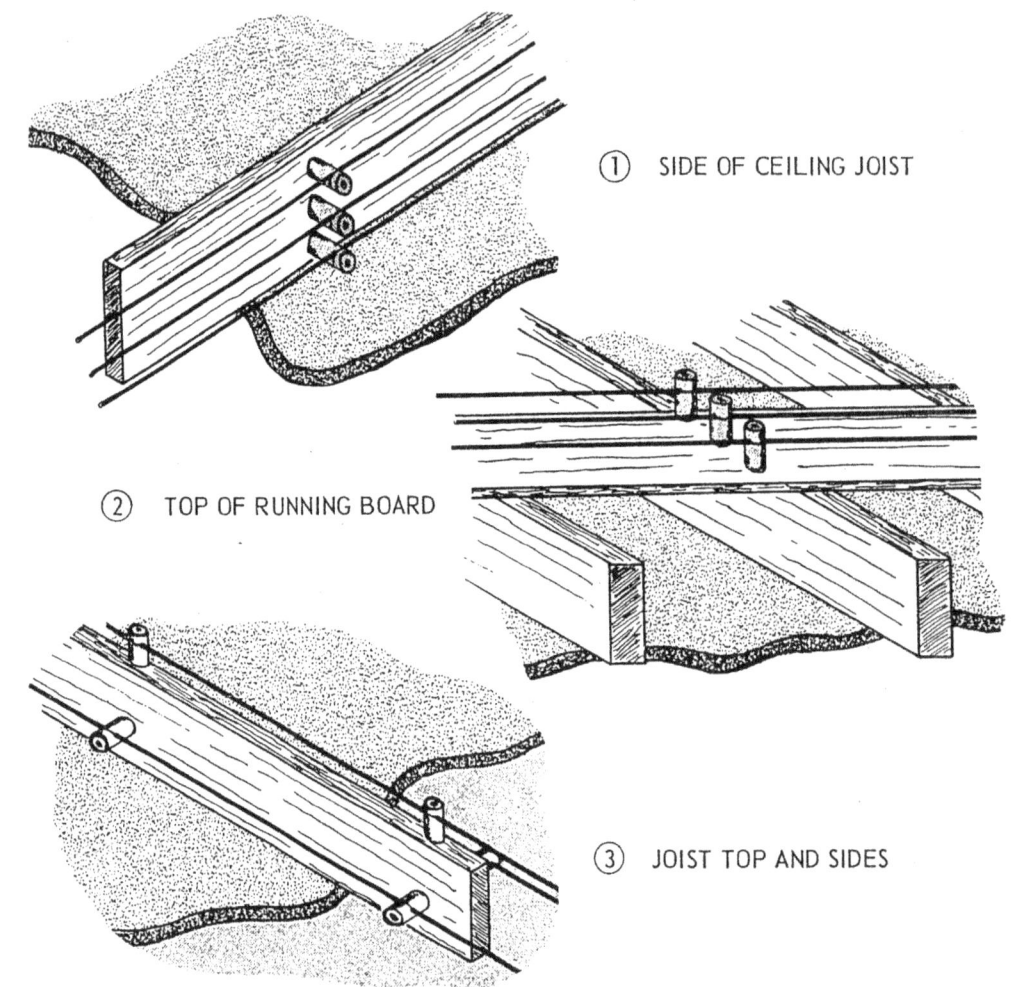

Figure 66. Knob mounting for three-wire circuits.

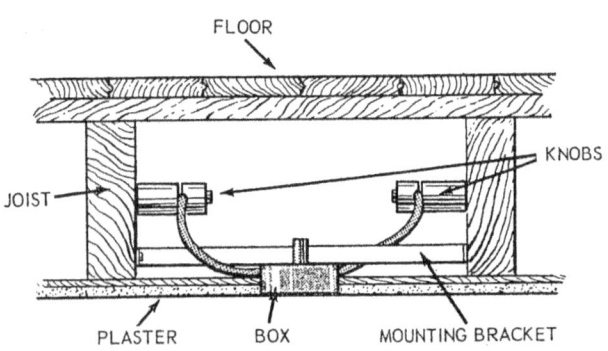

Figure 67. Installation of box in plaster.

d. Figure 71 illustrates a typical service-entrance installation and figure 72 shows the procedures in circuit breaker wiring. If a service-entrance switch were used instead of a main circuit breaker, a separate fuse cabinet would be required to provide individual circuit protection. The wires from the powerline should be secured to the building at least 10 feet from the ground for normal installations. When the service entrance is located above a roadway this height should be increased to 18 feet. If the building is not high enough to meet these requirements, the entrance height may be less, provided all conductors within 8 feet of the ground are rubber-insulated. The line wires at the service entrance to a building should be spaced at least 6 inches apart and should be supported at least 2 inches from the building by service-entrance insulators or brackets. Upon entering the building, the line wires should be threaded upward through slanting noncombustible tubes so that moisture will not follow the conductor into the service-entrance switch.

e. Motors are often located with permanent power leads of exposed open wiring, requiring extensive damage protection. To minimize both time and expense the tap from the open-wiring ceiling circuits should be made with armored cable or conduit. Figure 73 shows a diagrammatic installation of the power connections and operating switch for a three-phase motor connected to exposed knob-and-tube wiring.

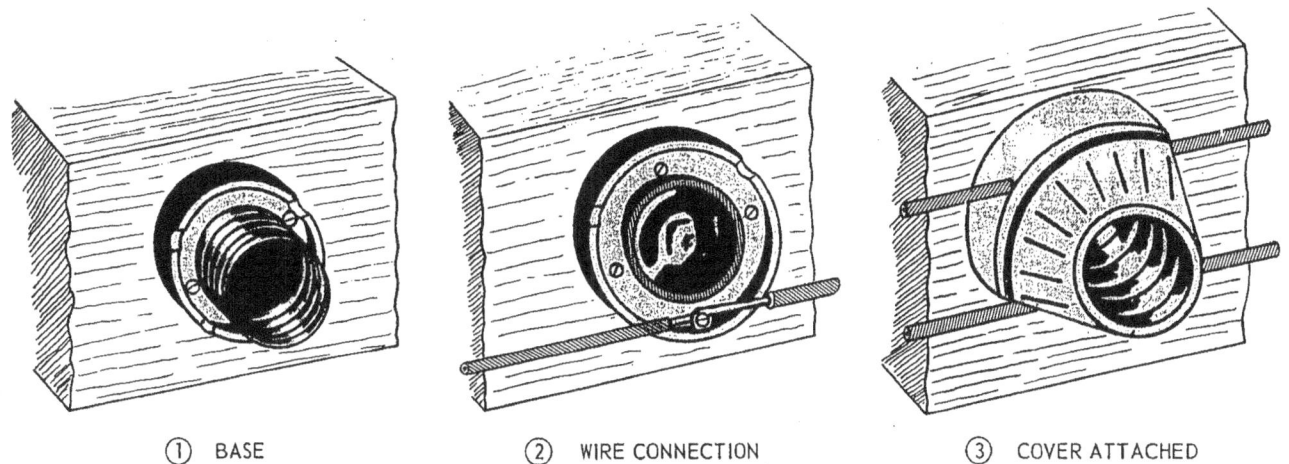

① BASE   ② WIRE CONNECTION   ③ COVER ATTACHED

Figure 68. Porcelain fittings used with knob and tube wiring.

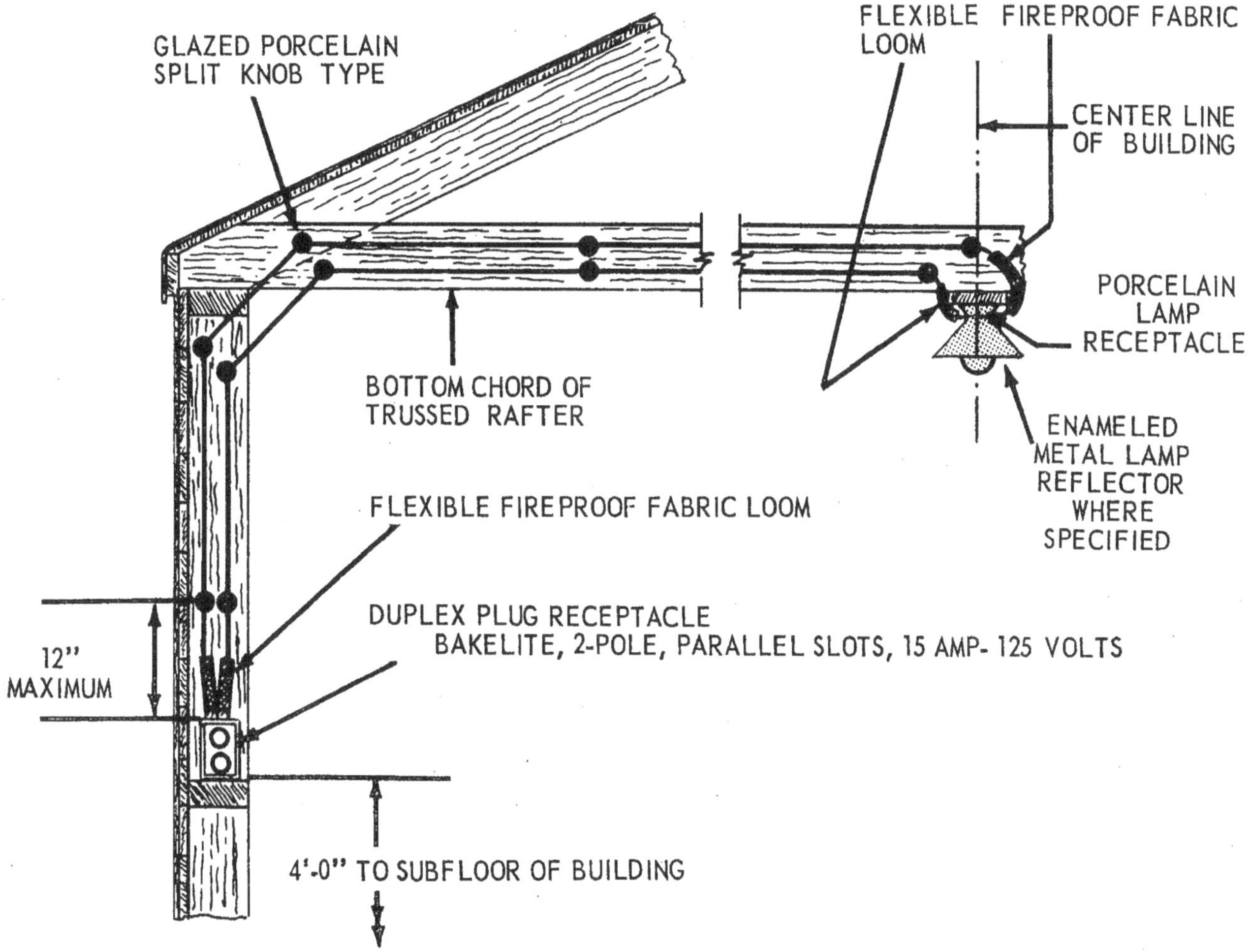

Figure 69. Typical duplex receptacle installation.

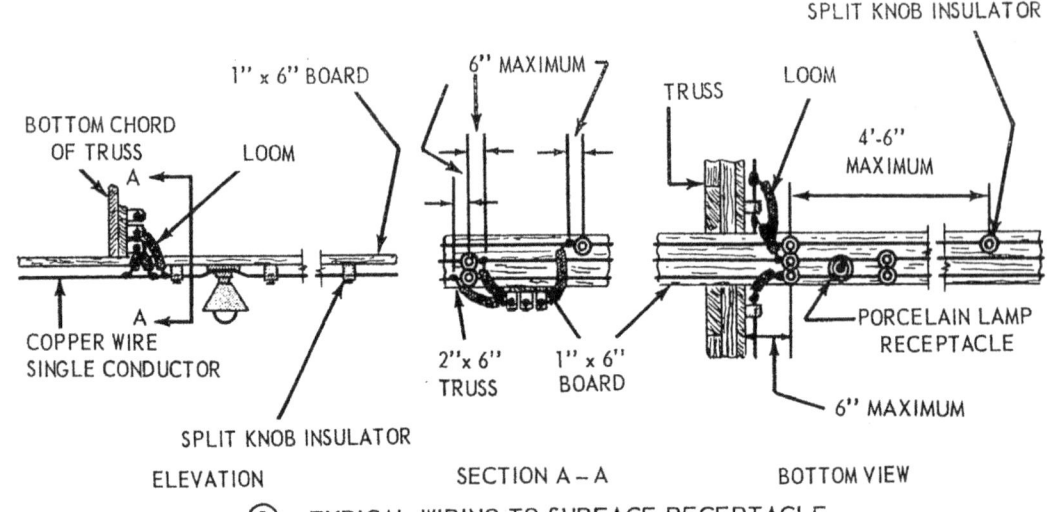
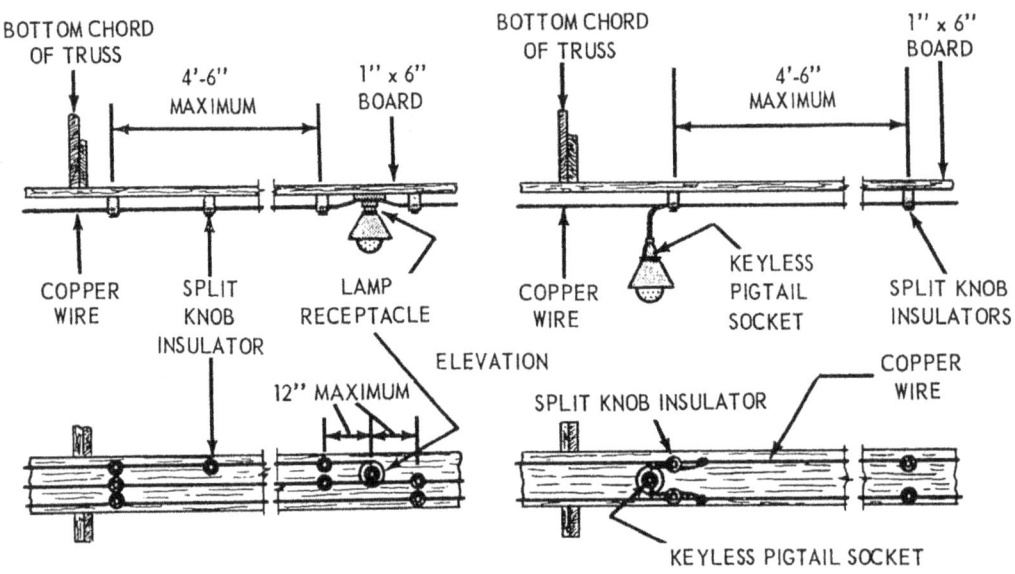
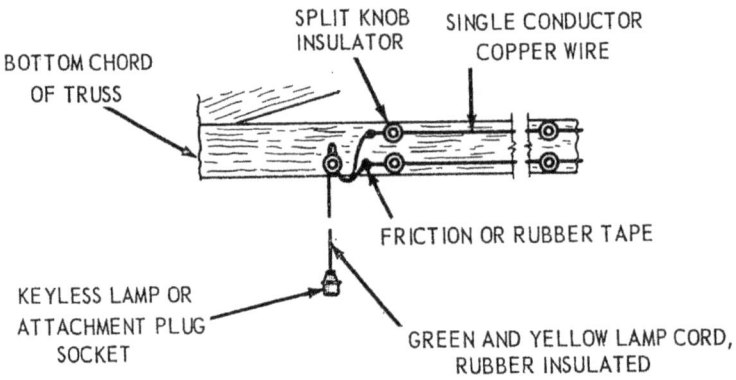

Figure 70. Lampholder installations.

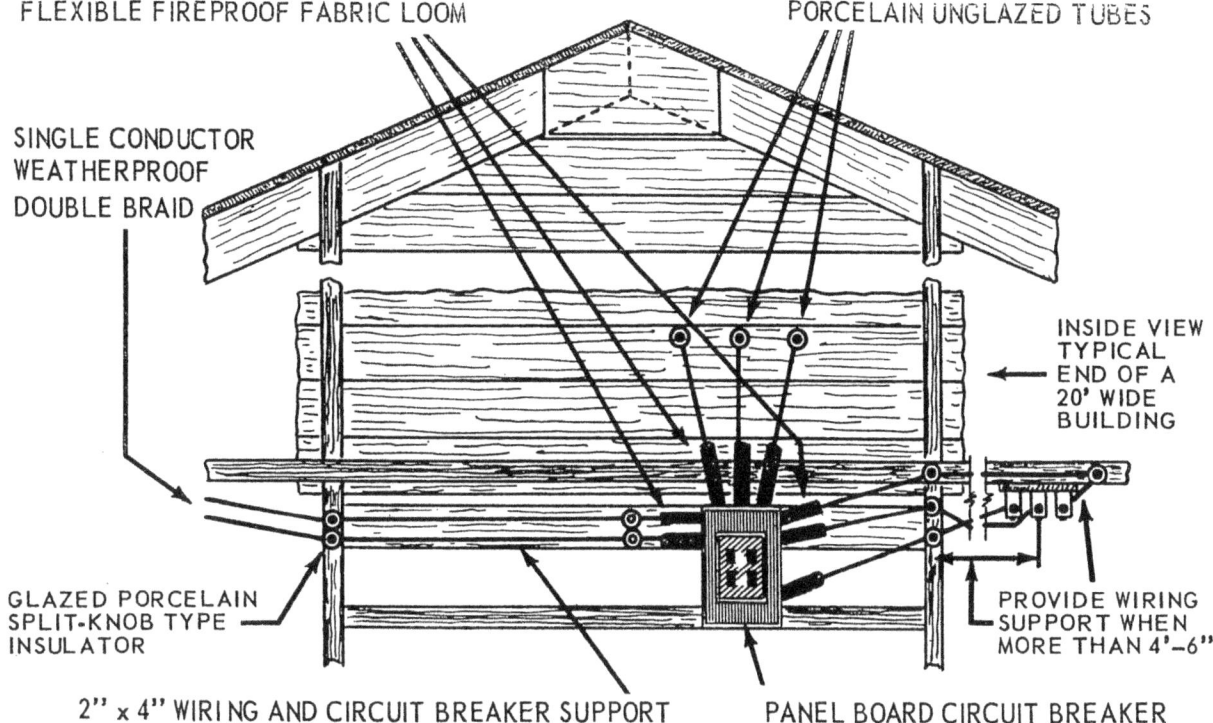

Figure 71. Typical main circuit breaker installation.

72. Additions to Existing Wiring

a. Circuiting. Additions to existing circuits require analysis to determine whether additional circuit capacity is needed to handle the new load. These considerations are the same as those required for other types of installations and are outlined in paragraph 55.

b. Wire Connection.

(1) *Where to connect.* An open wiring system has a distinct advantage over the other wiring methods in that wires for new or additional outlets can be attached to the circuit runs by merely making tap splices in the wire runs, or by extending the circuit from an outlet box. However, the electrician in planning these additional outlets in the existing circuits should be careful to have the shortest possible wire runs. This will result in attaining the lowest voltage drop.

(2) *How to connect.* First make sure the circuit is dead. This is a primary safety rule for all electricians working in existing wiring systems. This can be done by removing the fuse, tripping the circuit breaker to the OFF position, or pulling the service-entrance switch and disconnecting the entire building from power before commencing work. A voltage tester or test lamp is also used to doublecheck the circuit upon which work is to be done. The wires must then be connected and supported in the same manner as outlined for an original building installation.

c. Connections to Other Types of Wiring. Conduit and cable wiring cannot be installed with splices in the conduit or cable runs. Consequently, all splicing and connections must be made within the confines of an outlet, junction, or fuse box. Therefore, when open wiring is combined with one of the other wiring systems the transition from one system to another must be made in one of these boxes. Since standard outlet, junction, or fuse boxes are used, open wiring must be encased in loom at the box entry. An example combining knob-and-tube wiring and conduit wiring is illustrated in figure 74.

Section II. EXPEDIENT WIRING

73. Use

There are many applications where electrical wiring installations are needed for temporary use. One example is a forward area installation. A complete installation including knobs, tubes, cleats, and damage protection would require too much time and would be impractical. Consequently, expedient wir-

119

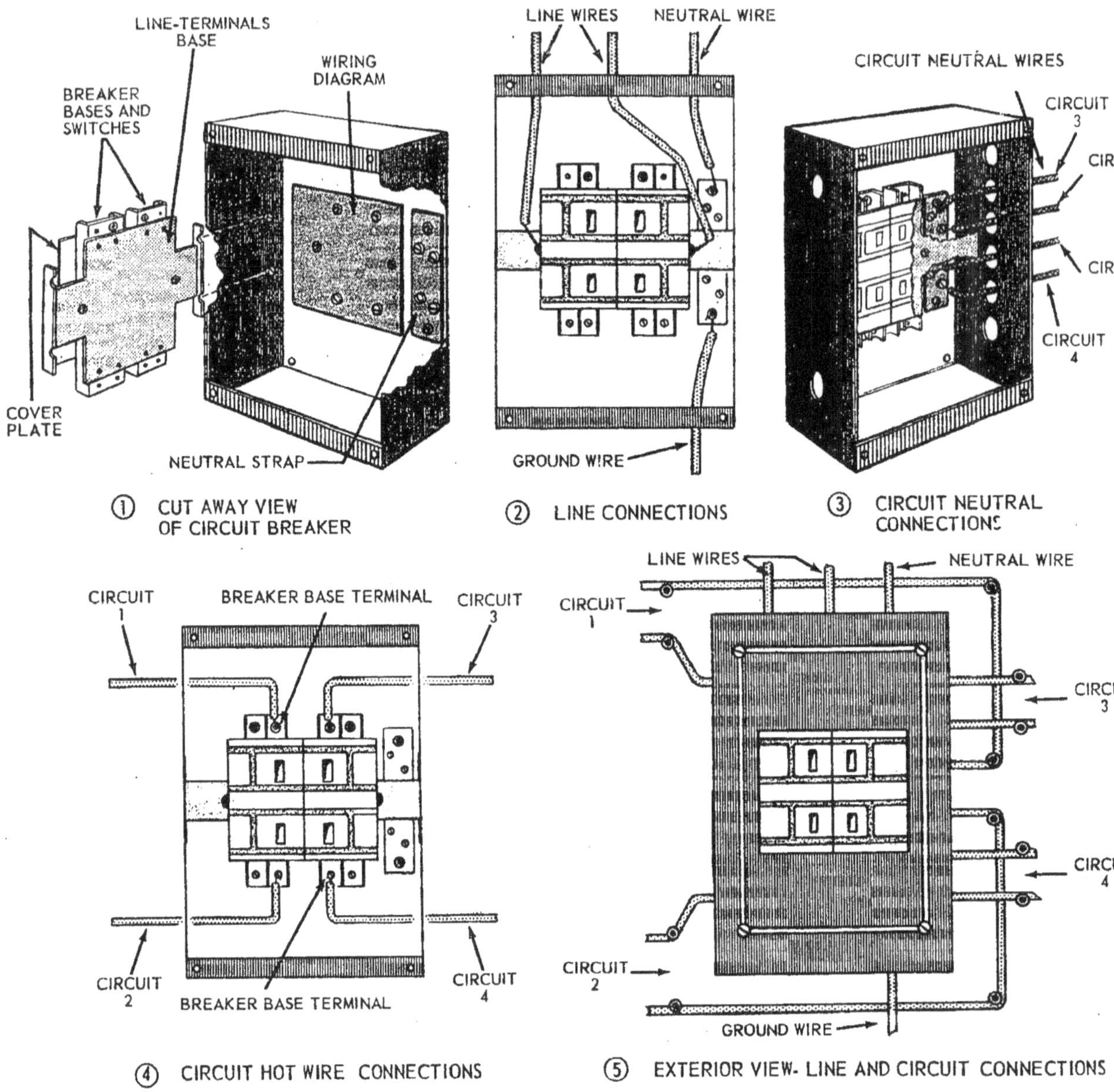

Figure 72. Typical circuit breaker wiring.

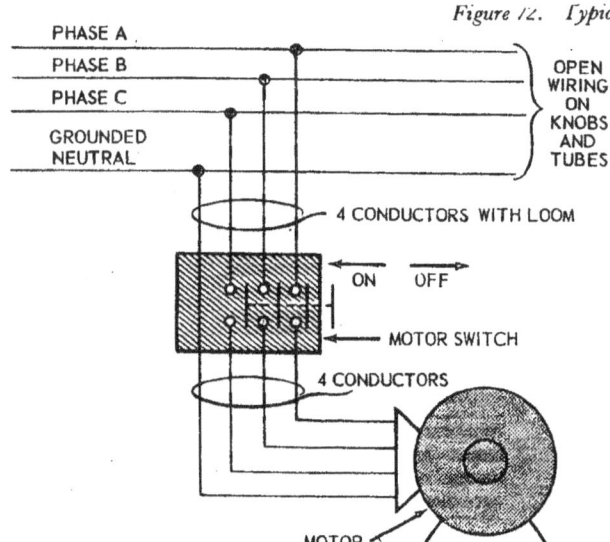

Figure 73. Motor connection.

ing used for temporary buildings and forward areas does not require the mounting and protective devices described in paragraphs 66 through 72. Generally the wires are attached to building members with nails, and pigtail sockets are used for outlets.

74. Installation

a. *Wire.*

(1) *Supports.* The wire sizes should be selected in accordance with normal installations. The wires should be laid over ceiling joists and fastened by nails driven into the joists and then bent over the wire as shown in figure 75. The nails should exert enough force to firmly grip the wire without injuring the insulation. If loom is available, it

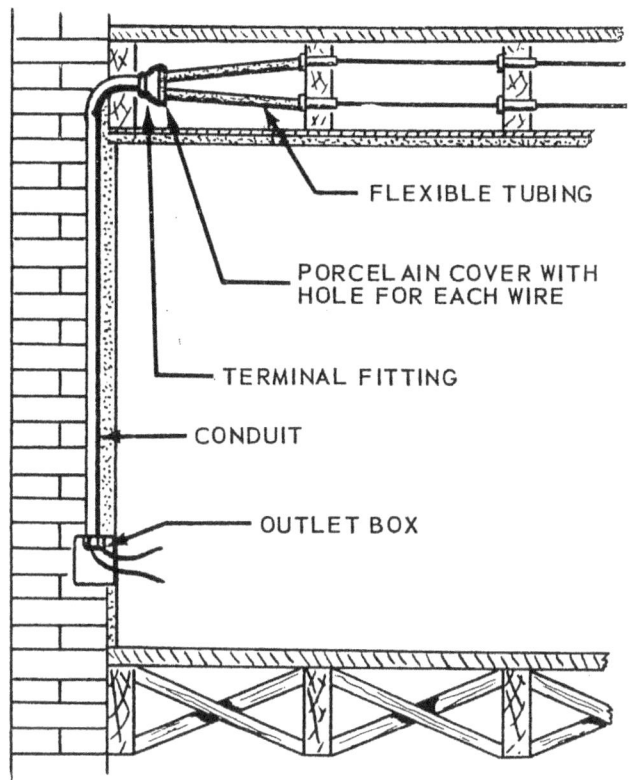

Figure 74. Changing from knob-and-tube to conduit wiring.

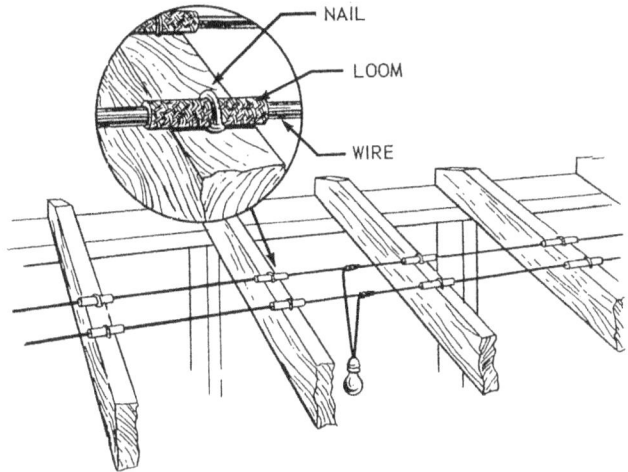

Figure 75. Expedient wiring.

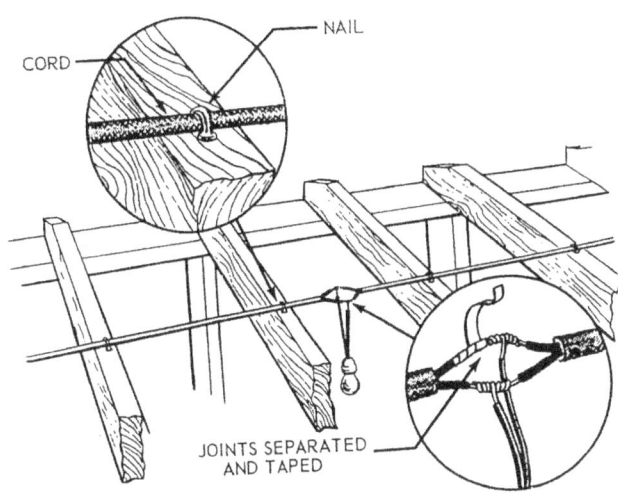

Figure 76. Expedient-wiring cord installation.

should be installed to protect the wire at the nail support. This is particularly essential if the wooden joists are wet. If possible, expedient wiring installations should be fastened to joists or studs at a distance of at least 7 feet above the floor. This will prevent accidental injury to the system or personnel which might result from the absence of damage protection.

(2) *Spacing.* The spacing of wires should be the same as that outlined for exposed knob and tube wiring.

(3) *Joints, splices, and taps.* Joints, splices, taps, and connections are made as outlined in paragraphs 60 through 65 with the exception of the procedures outlined for soldering and taping. In expedient wiring, soldering is omitted and only friction tape is used as a protective covering on the connections.

(4) *Fixture drops.* Fixture drops, preferable pigtail sockets, are installed by tapping their leads to wires, as shown in figure 75, and then taping the taps. The sockets are supported by the tap wires.

b. Cord. Figure 76 illustrates the application of a two-conductor cord in an expedient-wiring installation. The cord used should always be of the rubber-covered type and fastened securely to prevent the possibility of short circuits. The outer rubber sheathing should be removed at the point of fixture attachment and the fixture leads tapped into the conductor, purposely maintaining the separation between taps as shown. Each tap then should be individually taped.

Section III. BELL WIRING

75. Installation

Signal equipment may occasionally be supplied for 110-volt operation, in which case it must be installed in the same manner as outlets and sockets operating on this voltage. Most bells and buzzers are rated to operate on 8, 12, 18, or 24 volts ac or dc. These operating voltages are known as low-voltage or low-energy circuits. They can be installed with minimum consideration for circuit insulation since there is no danger of shock to personnel or fire due to short circuits. The wire commonly used is insulated with several layers of paraffin impregnated cotton or with a thermoplastic covering. Upon installation, these wires are attached to building members with small insulating staples and are threaded through building construction members without insulators.

76. Battery Operation

Early installations of low-voltage signal systems were powered by 6-volt dry cells. For example, 2 of these batteries were installed in series to service a 12-volt system. If the systems involved a number of signals over a large area, 1 or more batteries were added in series to offset the voltage drop. Though this type of alarm or announcing system is still being used and installed in some areas, it is a poor method because the batteries used as a power source require periodic replacement.

77. Transformer Operation

The majority of our present-day buzzer and bell signal systems operate from a transformer power source. The transformers are equipped to be mounted on outlet boxes and are constructed so that the 110-volt primary-winding leads normally extend from the side of the transformer adjacent to box mounting. These leads are permanently attached to the 110-volt power circuits, and the low-voltage secondary-winding leads of the transformer are connected to the bell circuit in a manner similar to a switch-and-light combination. If more than 1 buzzer and push button is to be installed they are paralleled with the first signal installation. A typical wiring schematic diagram for this type of installation is shown in figure 77.

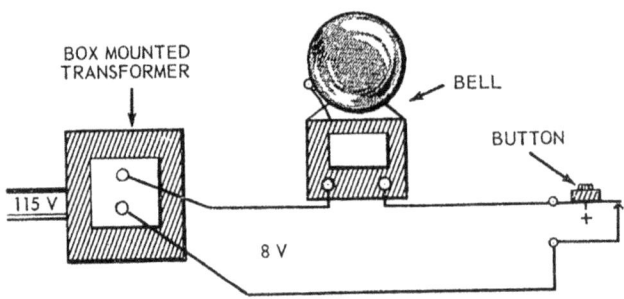

Figure 77. Bell and buzzer wiring.

www.ingramcontent.com/pod-product-compliance
Lightning Source LLC
Chambersburg PA
CBHW081828300426
44116CB00014B/2515